EASTERN FRONT

THE UNPUBLISHED PHOTOGRAPHS 1941–1945

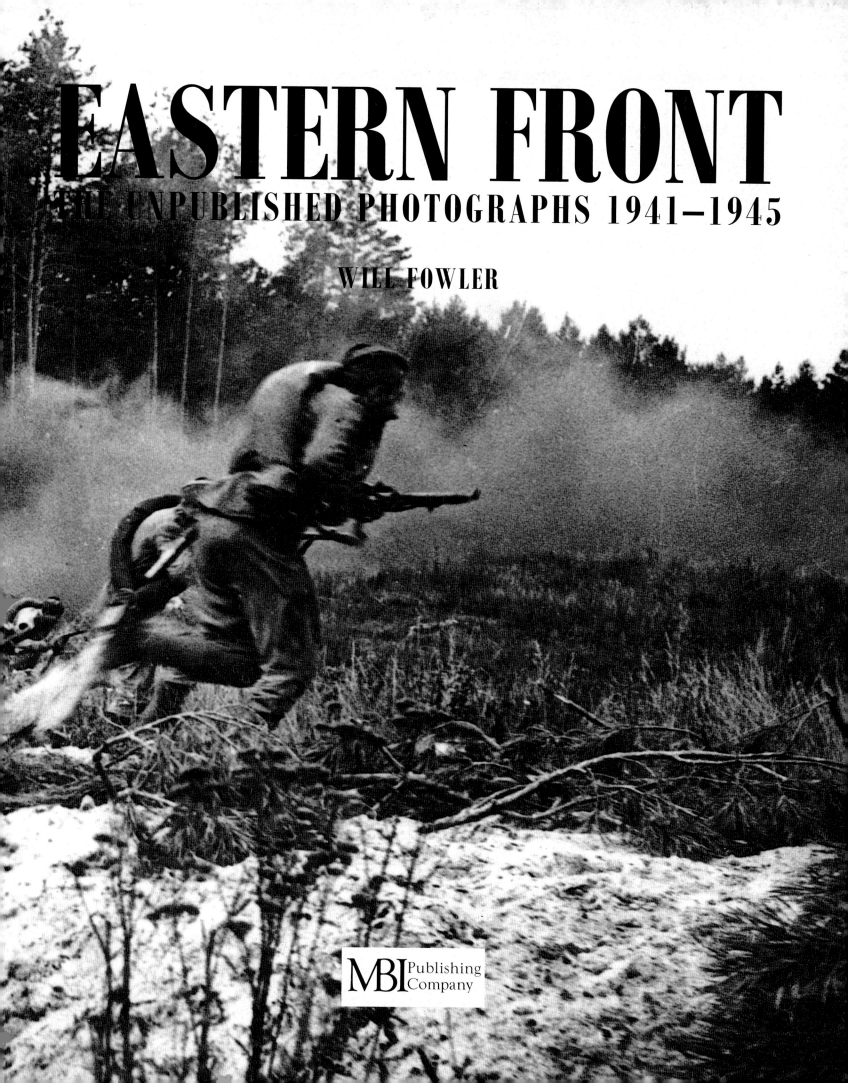

EASTERN FRONT

THE UNPUBLISHED PHOTOGRAPHS 1941–1945

WILL FOWLER

MBI Publishing Company

This edition first published in 2001 by
MBI Publishing Company,
Galtier Plaza, Suite 200
380 Jackson Street
St. Paul, MN 55101 USA
www.motorbooks.com

MBI Publishing Company books are also available at discounts in bulk quantity
for industrial or sales-promotional use. For details write to Special Sales Manager
at Motorbooks International Wholesalers & Distributors, Galtier Plaza,
Suite 200, 380 Jackson Street, St. Paul, MN 55101 USA.

Library of Congress Cataloging-in-Publication Data available.

ISBN 0-7603-1116-1

Editorial and design: Amber Books Ltd
Bradley's Close, 74-77 White Lion Street,
London N1 9PF

Project Editor: Charles Catton
Editor: Vanessa Unwin
Design: Kathy Ward and Brian Rust
Picture Research: Stasz Gnych
Caption Translation: Lisa Mazura

Printed and bound in Italy by: Eurolitho S.p.A., Cesano Boscone (MI)

Picture credits
All photographs Ukrainian State Archive except pages 6–10 inclusive (TRH Pictures)

CONTENTS

CHAPTER ONE

The Clash of Ideologies

The Opening Moves

It was, at the very least, a startling surprise; at worst, it was nothing short of a shocking betrayal.

On 20 August 1939, the German Führer, Adolf Hitler, leader of Germany's National Socialist (Nazi) Party, sent a telegram to Joseph Stalin, the Soviet Union's head of state, to urge an agreement because of the *'worsening situation in Poland'*.

Three days later, the Russo–German Pact was signed in Moscow by the German Foreign Minister, Joachim von Ribbentrop, and Soviet Minister, Viacheslav Molotov.

For the Nazis, the Russian Communists and their 'Bolshevik' followers in Europe had, from the outset, been the ultimate enemy. Now, ordinary Nazis were confused and conservative Germans shocked. Communists in Europe, many of whom had fought fascism in Spain, were equally shaken by the unexpected agreement.

In his speeches and writings in the 1920s and 1930s, Hitler, who had taken power and established the Third Reich in 1933, rolled anti-Semitism and hatred of Bolshevism into ranting outbursts that enraptured his audiences in Germany. The Communists were the enemies who had destroyed Germany in World War I and impoverished it in the 1920s, and now plotted to corrupt and enslave Europe. In his political testament, *Mein Kampf (My Struggle)*, he wrote:

It must never be forgotten that the present rulers of Russia are blood-stained criminals, that here we have the dregs of humanity which, favoured by the circumstances of a tragic moment, overran a great State, degraded and extirpated millions of educated people out of sheer blood-lust, and that now for nearly ten years they have ruled with such a savage tyranny as was never known before. It must not be forgotten that the international Jew, who is today the absolute master of Russia, does not look upon

LEFT: Nazi Foreign Minister von Ribbentrop watches as his Soviet counterpart, Molotov, signs the Non-Aggression Pact in August 1939.

FAR LEFT: Adolf Hitler, Führer (Leader) of Nazi Germany who, seeing Communism as his implacable enemy, would unleash Operation Barbarossa on the USSR.

Germany as an ally, but as a State condemned to the same doom as Russia.

STORM TROOPS

In the 1920s, during the time of the Weimar Republic, the Nazi *Sturmabteilung* (SA), or Storm Troops, fought street battles with a paramilitary organisation known by the name of the *Rotfrontkämpferbund* (RFB), which was the Red Frontline Fighters' League of the *Kommunistische Partei Deutschlands* (KPD), the German Communist Party. Fear of Marxism and anti-Semitism were both fuelled by the Jewish origins of revolutionaries such as Leon Trotsky, born Lev Davidov Bronstein, and German-born Karl Marx, whose family had converted to Christianity from Judaism. After the end of World War I, revolution in Russia and left-wing revolts in Germany, the *Dolchstosstheorie* ('Stab in the Back' theory) asserted that Germany had been destroyed from within – with the blame being levelled firmly at 'Jews, traitors and Social Democrats'. Rosa Luxemburg in Berlin and Kurt Eisner in Munich, both murdered in 1919 because they were Bolsheviks urging revolutionary change, were subsequently portrayed as anti-German Jewish agitators.

Although the Russo–German Pact of August 1939 may well have shocked Nazis and severely tested the loyalty of Communists worldwide, it did pave the way for the Russo–German invasion of Poland in September. It ensured that:

RIGHT: Storm Troopers, the political muscle of the nascent Nazi Party, pose in a beer hall in the 1920s. Drawing their membership from ex-soldiers and the unemployed, they were happy to blame the Communists for the defeat in World War I and subsequent unemployment in the Weimar Republic. When the Nazis came to power in 1933 – after the political anarchy of the 1920s – they were quick to sack the Communist Party offices in Germany.

Neither party would attack the other. Neither party would in any manner lend its support to a third power, should the other party become the object of belligerent action by that third power.

Neither Germany nor Russia would join any grouping of Powers whatsoever which was aimed directly or indirectly at the other party.

THE SECRET PROTOCOL

A secret protocol was attached to the pact. It identified spheres of interest in Poland and the Baltic: the USSR had claims on Finland, Estonia, Latvia and Lithuania, with the northern border of Lithuania as a diving line. In Poland, Soviet influence would reach as far as the line of the rivers Narew, Vistula and San. In a piece of brutal strategic pragmatism, Hitler had ensured that the USSR would not intervene to support the Poles. However, the attack on Poland committed France and Britain, who had guaranteed to support the Poles, to declaring war on Germany.

Since the Munich Agreement of 1938, Britain, France and Poland, linked by the common threat of Nazi Germany, had begun work on breaking the signals produced by German Enigma code machines. The Enigma was a highly sophisticated mechanical encryption system used in radio transmissions and one which the Germans firmly believed was completely secure. The secrecy for the Enigma project was at such a high level that it was classified by the British as 'Ultra Secret' and so became known as ULTRA.

LEFT: The then British Prime Minister, Neville Chamberlain, examines some of the documents drafted at the Munich on 30 September 1938 between Germany, Italy, France and Britain, which ceded the German-speaking Sudetenland of Czechoslovakia to Germany. In August, Hitler had mobilised his army and threatened to attack the Czechs. Condemned as 'appeasement' by many such as Winston Churchill, the Munich Agreement actually bought time for Britain in which it could begin to re-arm and prepare for war.

ULTRA was still in its infancy in the autumn of 1939 and could not save Poland. In four weeks, the invading German armies, consisting of the 3rd and 4th Armies of Army Group North under General Fedor von Bock, and the 8th, 10th and 14th Armies of Army Group South under General Gerd von Rundstedt, had defeated the Poles. Poland's final collapse was accelerated, however, by the Red Army's invasion and seizure of its eastern territories on 17 September. The Russo-German Pact allowed the Germans to carve Poland in half with the USSR and also gave the Soviet giant a free hand in the Baltic.

Even before the pact had been signed with Germany, the USSR had enjoyed good, if covert, relations with the Reichswehr, Germany's military forces from 1919 to 1935. Following the Treaty of Versailles, Germany was limited to an army of 100,000 men and a navy of 15,000, while an air force was forbidden. The secret links it enjoyed with the Red Army meant that, from 1924, Reichswehr tank crews were training in the USSR and, from 1930, their air crews were practising bombing techniques.

On 30 November 1939, the USSR invaded Finland. Stalin had already established with von Ribbentrop that the Baltic States of Latvia, Lithuania and Estonia were in the Soviet sphere of influence. In October 1939, a 'mutual assistance pact' had been agreed between the USSR and Latvia. In June 1940, while the world watched the German invasion of the West, the USSR effortlessly gathered up the three tiny states.

THE COMMUNIST ENEMY

Finland, however, was a different customer. Stalin saw the close proximity of the fortified Finnish border close to Leningrad, the USSR's second city, as a threat. He offered a mutual assistance treaty and demanded that Finland cede the area known as the Karelian Isthmus to the USSR. Finland refused on both counts and, on 30 November 1939, the Soviets invaded. In the bitter winter, 15 Finnish divisions inflicted a heavy defeat on 45 Soviet divisions that had attacked overland and in three amphibious operations. On 5 January 1940, at Suomussalmi in Karelia, outnumbered Finnish ski troops counterattacked the Soviet 163rd and 44th divisions and destroyed them. The German staff officers watched the Soviets' incompetence and concluded that the

BELOW: German troops take cover in the fighting for Warsaw during the September 1939 invasion of Poland. The Polish capital fell on 27 September; the last vestige of resistance ended by 5 October. The campaign had cost the Germans 8082 killed, 27,278 wounded and 5029 missing. Polish casualties were 70,000 killed and 130,000 wounded. The campaign's speed and its low cost to the Germans in casualties was in part the result of the Soviet attack on eastern Poland.

USSR would be easy meat for their Panzer divisions and *Blitzkrieg* tactics.

The poor performance of the Red Army was in part the result of Stalin's purges. In 1938, in a frenzy of paranoia, Stalin ordered show trials be held in Moscow, in which some 10,000 senior officers were accused of treachery. Almost all 'confessed', were found guilty and were executed. The Red Army lost many experienced and talented commanders.

Despite heavy losses, the massively reinforced North-West Front, composed of the 7th and 13th Armies under General Merestokov, punched through the defences of the Mannerheim Line. Finland was crushed by sheer weight of numbers and forced to capitulate on 12 March 1940. The war had cost the Russians 200,000 men, nearly 700 aircraft and 1600 tanks. The Finns, in contrast, lost 25,000 men.

LEBENSRAUM

The German war with the USSR had long been predicted. For Hitler, the drive on the east would give the Germans *Lebensraum* ('living space'), the slogan of expansionism that had come into use in the late nineteenth century as Imperial Germany worked to create a colonial empire. It was a concept that Hitler had first proposed in *Mein Kampf*. He believed that Germany was overpopulated and needed more land to support that population. Poland and Russia were the new territories where his vision of *Lebensraum* could become a reality.

Despite this, throughout the winter of 1939–40 and the following summer, the USSR abided by its treaty obligations to Germany. When Germany invaded Western Europe in May 1940, it did so fed and fuelled by Soviet wheat and oil.

ABOVE: Crowds in Danzig (now Gdansk) greet a German artillery regiment as it rumbles by in half-tracks towing 15cm (5.9in) guns. The reoccupation of the pre-1919 German-owned port was, like the earlier occupations of the Rhineland, Austria and part of the Sudetenland, extremely popular with most of the ethnic German civilians who lived there.

RIGHT: Soldiers of the 123rd Lenin Banner Infantry Division, one of the units that penetrated the Mannerheim Line. At the front are two officers, the older man on the left wearing the *shlem* peaked cap is probably the division's *politicheskii rukovoditel* (political officer), its *Politruk* or *Kommissar* (Commissar). The role of political officers was partly party political spy, trying to ensure that officers remained loyal to the Communist Party, but they were also given the task of looking after the wellbeing of the troops in the front line.

BELOW: Soviet troops at a railway station in Manchuria in 1929. The border with Japanese-occupied Manchuria was garrisoned by large and well-equipped forces on both sides and it was always an area of high tension. For the Soviet forces, there was the humiliating memory of defeat in the Russo–Japanese War of 1904–05. In September 1939, the then little-known General Georgi Zhukov inflicted a sharp defeat on the Japanese Kwantung Army at Khalkin-Gol in Outer Mongolia.

LEFT: Soviet soldiers in an exposed trench in the Finnish campaign of 1939–40. The defences do not appear to have any barbed wire obstacles or bunkers for protection against artillery fire. The soldiers are armed with the 7.62mm (0.3in) Mosin Nagant M1891/30 bolt-action rifle. The rifle had a fixed hinged-spike bayonet that folded back against the barrel. They wear the M1936 *stalnoi shlem* (steel helmet), but their *shinel* (greatcoats) would offer poor protection against the Arctic cold.

BELOW: After breaking through the Mannerheim Line, a Red Army machine-gun crew engages the outnumbered Finnish forces near Viborg. The weapon is a Maxim 1910, a water-cooled machine gun that had a rate of fire of 550 rounds per minute. On its wheeled Sokolov mount, with its shield, it weighed a staggering 74kg (163lb). The original version of the gun adopted by the Russians in 1905 had a bronze water jacket, but this was replaced by a steel corrugated one in 1910.

RIGHT: Soviet artillery fire falls on a Finnish position. The position is probably the Mannerheim Line, the defences that ran from Lake Ladoga to the Gulf of Finland and protected Finland's left flank. They were finally penetrated in March 1940 at considerable cost to the Soviet 13th and 7th Armies, and that month a peace was signed between Finland and the USSR. The Soviet attack on Finland, a small neutral country, caused international outrage and led to the expulsion of the USSR from the League of Nations.

ABOVE: Dressed in white snow camouflage, a Soviet patrol sets off during the Russo–Finnish War. Finnish ski troops were far more effective with these tactics and earned the nickname *Bielaya Smert* ('White Death'). Their major triumph was against the Soviet 163rd and 44th Divisions at Suomussalmi, where, in the snow-covered forest, they ambushed and destroyed the poorly led and badly equipped Soviet forces. Soviet losses in the Russo–Finnish war included 1600 tanks – the Finns none.

CHAPTER TWO

Barbarossa

The Drive on the East

In the spring of 1941, Stalin chose to ignore the indicators he was receiving that German forces were massing on the Russo-Polish border, feeling secure, perhaps, in the belief that the Russo–German Pact still held. He may well not have wished to provoke Hitler or perhaps he believed that the Führer would not start a war in the East while Britain

LEFT: Germans soldiers rest outside a captured bunker in the Ukraine in 1941, part of the Stalin Line, the fixed defences that had been built in the Soviet Union before 1939.

FAR LEFT: A female orderly of the Soviet Army Medical service tends the leg wound of a German *Obergefreiter* (senior corporal) in July 1941.

remained undefeated in the West. War on two fronts had always been a recipe for disaster.

Among the indicators that Stalin chose to overlook were the improvement and development of road and rail links through Eastern Europe leading to the borders of the USSR under the Otto Programme. 'Otto' stood for *Ost* (east) and the programme that had been initiated on 1 October 1940 was completed on 10 May 1941, in preparation for the attack.

TOKYO SPY

In Tokyo, Richard Sorge, a German Communist and an agent of the Soviet Army intelligence service, the *Glavnoye Razvedyvatel'noye Upravleniye* (GRU, or Central Intelligence Administration), was working undercover as a loyal Nazi and a journalist for the *Frankfurter Zeitung*. There, he learned about Operation Barbarossa four months before the attack and duly warned the Russians. In Germany, from 1938, the *Rote Kapelle* (the Red Orchestra), the largest spy and resistance organisation within Germany and occupied Europe, had been passing information to Moscow. Even though it stood down between 1939 and 1941, it, too, had warned Stalin. Finally, if the Soviet leader had studied *Mein Kampf*, he would have read Hitler's comment that: 'Any alliance whose purpose is not the intention to wage war is senseless and useless.'

The invasion of Russia at dawn on 22 June 1941 therefore – literally – caught the Russians napping. Border guards were

captured semi-clothed, as they stumbled half-awake out of their barracks. Army propaganda photographers caught the dazed look on their shocked faces in the watery spring light.

The invasion plans had been drafted as far back as 6 December 1940, with the code name *Fall Fritz* (Plan Fritz). However, on 18 December, Hitler changed the name to *Unternehmen Barbarossa* (Operation Barbarossa, or the Emperor known as 'Red Beard', the hero of the Holy Roman Empire who led the Third Crusade and died in Asia Minor). Hitler assured his generals that: 'When Barbarossa begins, the world will hold its breath and say nothing.'

THREE ARMY GROUPS

In June 1941, German troops with their Romanian, Finnish, Hungarian and Italian allies began to turn these ideas into reality as they punched eastwards, deep into the Soviet Union. The attack was split between three Army Groups. Army Group North under Field Marshal Ritter von Leeb consisted of seven divisions and three panzer divisions; Army Group Centre under Field Marshal Fedor von Bock was made up of 42 divisions and nine panzer divisions; and Army Group South under Field Marshal Gerd von Rundstedt was made up of 52 divisions, of which 15 were Romanian, two Hungarian, and two Italian, plus five Panzer Divisions. The army groups were supported by nine lines of communications divisions and more than 3000 aircraft.

ABOVE: Aware that, as reservists, they are liable for service, male civilians in Kiev listen to an announcement made by the Soviet *Informburo* on the national radio on 22 June 1941. They have just learned that German forces have invaded the USSR. The tanks of Field Marshal Ewald von Kleist's 1st Panzer Group, part of Army Group South, soon reached the city.

The Soviet forces opposite them were grouped in three army groups known as 'fronts' – the North-Western, the Western and the South-West – and consisted of 158 divisions with 54 tank brigades. However, they had huge reserves and, within six months, 300 new divisions had been mobilised.

In the first few days of June 1941, the Luftwaffe destroyed 3000 aircraft in the air and on the ground, nearly half the Red Air Force. The tactical bombers attacked road and rail communications, destroyed headquarters and even bombed small targets such as bunkers and trench lines.

Although the opening months of the war in the East were a disaster for the Soviet Union and Stalin, geography favoured them. Whereas, in the West, the German Panzer divisions were able to advance on surfaced roads and the distances between objectives such as ports, airfields and cities were tens or hundreds of miles, in the USSR, roads that were dirt tracks linked cities vast distances apart. Dust, mud and, later, extreme cold would take a toll on men and machines. Photographs showed the dusty German *Landser* – 'Squaddies' or 'Grunts' – slogging through dust that would later turn to mud in the autumn and finally be covered in snow.

STALIN SPEAKS

On 3 July, Stalin broadcast to the people of the Soviet Union. At this low point in its fortunes, he assured his listeners: 'History shows us that there are no invincible armies.' As the British forces fighting Germany were severely stretched and the United States was not (yet) a belligerent in World War II, Communist Russia was welcomed by Winston Churchill as a new ally in the war against Nazi Germany.

The German Army would also not be well served by Hitler, who would increasingly interfere, reduce tactical flexibility and, as a result, cause needless casualties. Even before the operation was launched, there was a conflict of views among the German planners.

The first plan drafted by General Marcks, the Chief of Staff of the 18th Army, envisaged a twin thrust at Moscow and Kiev. A huge encircling battle could be fought as the Moscow thrust swung south to link up with the Kiev axis at Kharkov. General Halder, Chief of the OKW (*Oberkommando der Wehrmacht*, or the Armed Forces High Command), proposed an attack that spread the weight more equally between the north, centre and south, but which made Moscow

RIGHT: Luftwaffe Heinkel He 111 bombers during operations in the Ukraine in 1941. The He 111 could carry 2500kg (5511lbs) of bombs and had a maximum speed of 415km/h (258mph). Medium bombers such as the He 111 would attack headquarters, airfields and transportation to the rear of the enemy front line. At the front, fighters and dive-bombers such as the Ju-87 Stuka were used to destroy bunkers and artillery positions, and strafe infantry caught in the open.

the main objective. Hitler, however, proposed that Leningrad, 'the cradle of the Bolshevik revolution', should be the main objective and that Moscow should be taken subsequently.

Optimistic German planners envisaged holding the A–A line, from Archangel in the north to Astrakhan in the south, by the onset of winter 1941. Optimism and ignorance also featured in their assessment of the Russian winter. Men were woefully ill-equipped and, in the first winter, received no cold-weather uniforms, while the lubricants in engines and grease in their weapons thickened and froze. In the winter of 1941–42, the German Army suffered 133,620 frostbite casualties.

German tank and mechanised infantry in fast-moving Panzer divisions outmanoeuvred the Soviet armies, cut them off and surrounded them in huge pockets. By 9 July, the German and Axis advance had crossed the old 1939 Russo-Polish border, swallowed up Latvia, Lithuania and most of Estonia on the Baltic, and captured Minsk, where 300,000 Soviet soldiers were trapped. By 7 August, von Bock's Army Group Centre had captured 850,000 prisoners. By the end of September, the German armies had surrounded Leningrad, Odessa on the Black Sea and Sevastopol in the Crimea, and they held a line that ran almost due south from Lake Ladoga to the Sea of Azov. On 7 October, the trap closed on 650,000 Russian soldiers at Vyazma near Moscow. By the end of the year, 12 pockets, large and small, had been encircled and neutralised in western Russia and the Ukraine.

LEFT: Soviet soldiers man a quad 7.62mm (0.3in) Pulemet Maksima Obrazets 1910 Maxim machine gun on the roof of one of the apartment blocks overlooking Kharkov's Red Square in 1941. The fire from this AA configuration of the weapon would be 2080 to 2400 rounds a minute; however, even though the mount would take some of the weight, the gunner would still have to swing more than 95kg (209lb) of gun about as he followed the path of an enemy aircraft.

LEFT: The Junkers Ju 87 Stuka dive-bomber over the Ukraine in 1941. Armed with three or four 7.92mm (0.31in) machine guns and with a crew of two, it could carry up to 7000kg (15,432lbs) of bombs. Later in the war, the Ju-87G D-5 was armed with twin 3.7cm (1.45in) Flak 18 guns for use in an anti-tank role. The Ju-87D had a span of 13.8m (45ft), was powered by a 1043kW (1400hp) Jumo 211J engine and had a maximum speed of 410km/h (255mph). By late 1944, 5709 Stukas had been built.

LEFT: Soviet AA gunners man a camouflaged heavy M-1939 KS-12 85mm (3.35in) AA gun in the centre of Kharkov in the summer of 1941. Behind them are the huge apartment blocks built in the 1930s that surrounded the wide boulevards of the circular Red Square in the city.

The KS-12 had a maximum horizontal range of 15,650m (51,345ft) and a vertical range of 10,500m (34,450ft). An experienced crew could fire between 15 and 20 rounds per minute. In 1944, the KS-12 would be replaced in Soviet service by the improved KS-18.

RIGHT: Soviet Air Force armourers fuse 250kg (551lb) bombs for a Ilyushin DB-3F long-range bomber prior to a mission from an airfield in the Crimea in 1941. The twin 820kW (1100hp) M-88B engines gave the DB-3, also known as the Il-4, a top speed of 429km/h (267mph) at 6700m (21,982ft). The bombers were also used for carrying paratroops and as a glider tug, and the DB-PT was a torpedo bomber version carrying a 940kg (2072lb) torpedo under the fuselage.

BELOW: The crew of a M1939 KS-12 85mm (3.35in) AA gun prepare to engage ground targets during the fighting near Odessa in the summer of 1941. Firing armour-piercing high-explosive (APHE) ammunition, the KS-12 could penetrate 102mm (4in) of armour at 1000m (1094yds); with high-velocity armour piercing (HVAP), this rose to 130mm (5.1in). In many ways, the KS-12 and KS-18 were similar in performance to the German 8.8cm (3.45in) dual-purpose gun.

RIGHT: Soviet Air Force armourers break down the wooden packaging around 250kg (551lb) bombs before loading them onto a camouflaged Tupolev SB-2bis bomber on a grass strip in July 1941. Even before 1941, the SB-2 had already seen action. Some 200 operated with the Republican Air Force in the Spanish Civil War. The Soviet Union also used it to attack Helsinki in the Russo–Finnish war and it flew with the Nationalist Chinese in the Sino–Japanese wars.

RIGHT: A Polikarpov I-16 Type 10 fighter prepares for take off early in the war in Russia. It had a top speed of 460km/h (286mph) and was armed with two 7.62mm (0.3in) ShKAS machine guns and two 20mm (0.79in) ShVA cannon. The I-16 had already seen action in Spain and China, but suffered badly at the hands of the Luftwaffe. It did, however, later have some successes with air-to-air and air-to-ground rockets, and also equipped the first Soviet regiment to be elevated to Guards status.

ABOVE: A soldier of the 4th Shock Army of the Kalinin Front stands guard over a Messerschmitt Bf 109F fighter, which appears to have crash landed after air combat. The Bf 109F made up almost two-thirds of the Luftwaffe fighter force for the invasion of the Soviet Union. By the summer of 1941, some German pilots were veterans of almost three years of combat and quickly went into action, decimating the Soviet Air Force both in the air and on the ground.

RIGHT: Armoured train 'Letter A' of the People's Volunteer Corps, which is reported to have participated in the defence of Kiev in 1941. The barrels of heavy 12.7mm (0.5in) DSchK M38 machine guns can be seen protruding from the armoured sides of the car, while turreted guns are mounted on top. Each car in the train was a separate fighting unit, so that a fire or severe damage to one would not jeopardise the overall capabilities of the entire train.

BELOW: Festooned with ammunition and armed with a captured German bayonet, a Soviet officer shares a joke with men of his detachment who are about to be transported to rear areas.

ABOVE: 'Hedgehog' anti-tank obstacles were constructed from steel girders and were first developed by the Czechs before World War II. These have been positioned to block an approach to Kiev in late summer 1941. Hedgehogs were designed to wreck the tracks and running gear of a tank if it became impaled on them, or to simply present an obstacle an AFV could not push aside. The hedgehogs in this picture have been secured with concrete.

OPPOSITE LEFT: Soviet soldiers aboard camouflaged ZIS-6 trucks tow artillery away from Odessa in 1941. The city was besieged from 1 August 1941 and resisted for 73 days. The Black Sea Fleet landed 2000 Red Navy naval infantry or *Morskaia Pekhota* behind Romanian lines on 22 September, coordinated with a small parachute drop. The landings forced the Romanian forces to break off the siege. Between 1 and 16 October, the fleet evacuated 86,000 soldiers – who went on to fight at Sevastopol – and 15,000 civilians.

LEFT: A German PzKpfw IV Ausf E tank entering a populated village in the Cherkassy district of the Kiev region on 8 October 1941. This tank has extra armour added to the driver and bow gunner's positions, and spare track is attached to the glacis plate. The spare track gives added protection and, if the existing track is damaged, can be used for repairs in the field. The PzKpfw IV entered service in 1940 and would was in continued use until 1945 as a tank, while the chassis was also used for self-propelled guns and *Panzerjäger* (tank hunters).

BELOW: Ukrainians use horse-drawn *panje* wagons to make their escape from the advancing forces of Army Group South. The smoke on the horizon may not be from enemy action, but may have in fact been caused by the 'scorched earth' policy implemented on Stalin's orders, in which anything that might be of value to the invading enemy was wrecked, burned or blown up. Although many Germans were shocked at how ruthlessly this edict was carried out on their own country by the Red Army, they would themselves torch or demolish buildings and industrial plant as they withdrew in turn.

RIGHT: A 76.2mm (3in) Infantry Gun Model 1927 (76-27) of the South-Western Front commanded by D. Solodnov waits in ambush in September 1941. The gun was very successful. Weighing only 780kg (1720lb) in action, it fired a 6.21kg (13.7lb) shell to a maximum range of 8555m (9356yds). The gun stood 1321mm (4.3ft) high and was 3556mm (11.6ft) long. Large numbers were captured by the Germans, who went to the trouble of manufacturing ammunition for them and even fitting their own sights.

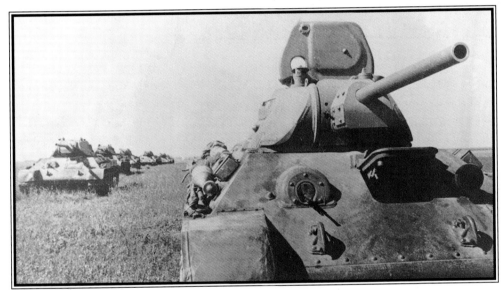

LEFT: A column of T-34/76B tanks commanded by Major Baranov waits in a holding area near the Crimea in October 1941. In many tanks, the driver had one of the most vulnerable positions if the tank was hit, since he was normally forced to climb back into the vehicle to exit via the turret hatches. In the T-34, the hatch on the glacis plate could be opened to give extra visibility when there was no threat or used for a quick exit.

RIGHT: A German machine-gun crew moves forwards with a *Sturmgeschütz* (assault gun) StuG III Ausf A during the battles in the eastern suburbs of Kiev on 8 October 1941. The StuG III Ausf A had a crew of four and was armed with a short-barrelled 7.5cm (2.9in) KwK L/24 gun, intended to give supporting fire for tanks or infantry. Less complex and costly to produce than a tank, assault guns were manufactured in ever greater numbers.

RIGHT: A small convoy including Communist Party functionaries or senior Soviet Army officers in two Russian-built GAZ-61 4x4 staff cars attempts to flee the German encirclement at Kiev in October 1941 and the subsequent drive eastwards to Kharkov. The staff cars are effectively five-seater civilian saloons – the GAZ-61 was capable of 100km/h (62mph) on roads. Later in the war, the Soviet Army received over 20,000 Lend-Lease Jeeps from the United States, massively enhancing its mobility.

BELOW: Civilian men and women digging an anti-tank ditch outside Kiev in the summer of 1941. Anti-tank ditches were normally a wedge shape, with a shallow slope towards the enemy and a near-vertical bank on the defender's side or a sharp 'V' shape. Ideally, enemy tank crews would not see the ditch and their vehicle would fall into it and become trapped, or would simply be unable to climb the steep far bank. Anti-tank guns would be sited to engage stalled enemy vehicles.

RIGHT: Cavalry units of the Soviet Army on the march in the Donetsk river region of the Dombass industrial area in the autumn of 1941. A pre-Revolutionary carriage has been pressed into service to provide transport for equipment and support weapons. The cavalry wear the stiff black burka cloak with its distinctive broad shoulders. Don Cossacks wore a tall, black fleece cap or *papkha*, while those from the Kuban and Terrek wore a shorter *kubanka* with a scarlet or blue top.

RIGHT: A Soviet locomotive burns on a railway bridge in the Ukraine on 20 October 1941. The train shows little battle damage that could have been caused by aircraft or gunfire, and may well have been positioned on the bridge in an attempt to deny it to the advancing German forces. For lack of explosives to destroy the steel girder bridge, the Soviet sappers may have sabotaged the engine. It was common practice to set fire to wooden bridges – although this might not destroy the target, it would weaken the structure.

LEFT: A broadside from the main armament of the battleship *Sevastopol*, firing in support of troops fighting near Odessa in October 1941. Shore bombardment, if properly coordinated, could be devastating, as between six and eight heavy-calibre shells could land on a target that was sometimes as small as a football pitch. However, this level of accuracy could only be achieved if a naval gunfire observer (NGO) was ashore and had a radio link to the battleship.

ABOVE: A M1939 KS-12 battery elevated for an attack by Luftwaffe aircraft in the autumn of 1941. On its platform, the gun had a 360-degree traverse and could elevate to 82 degrees and depress to minus 3 degrees. With its crew of seven, the gun could keep up a rate of fire of between 15 and 20 rounds a minute. The shallow angle of elevation of the guns suggests that they are preparing either to engage low-flying aircraft or a long-range target. Note the crew members ready with ammunition to reload.

LEFT: A Don Cossack cavalry officer stands with a group of Soviet soldiers by a captured and slightly battered PzKpfw IV Ausf F1. To Soviet tank crews, the German PzKpfw III and IV that were the mainstay of the German tank arm (*Panzerwaffe*) seemed to be slab-sided tanks that were much more vulnerable to hits by solid shot anti-tank rounds. The T-34 had a lower overall silhouette than the PzKpfw and its angled armour would often deflect shot.

ABOVE: Soldiers commanded by Captain A. P. Matukhin defending the Malakhov feature during the fighting for Sevastopol in the Crimea in November 1941. Although they all carry the PPSh-41 submachine gun, these men display an interesting mix of uniforms. Two wear the *shapka-ushanka* (the ear-flapped cap), while the man in the centre wears what appears to be a locally made hat and has a greatcoat with coloured collar patches indicating his branch within the army.

BELOW: Sergeant Dudchenko (on the right) prepares to give the order to fire to the crew of a captured German 10.5cm (4.13in) leFH 18 howitzer in November 1941. The leFH 18 weighed 1985kg (4376lb) in action and fired a 14.81kg (32.6lb) shell to a maximum range of 10,675m (11,674yds). It was developed in the late 1920s before the Nazis came to power and the first guns appeared in 1935. With some improvements, including weight reduction and increased range, it would serve until 1945.

CHAPTER THREE

Death in the Snow

Holding the Line at Moscow

By December 1941, the German forces had taken three and a third million prisoners, quite aside from the huge casualties they had inflicted on the Soviet Army. The German newspapers were filled with pictures of burning or wrecked vehicles, and with columns of tired, scruffy, starving prisoners plodding westwards. These were the *Untermenschen* (subhumans), the brutal racist name coined by the Nazis.

Now all that remained for the German forces was a final push to capture Moscow and, in Hitler's words at the beginning of Barbarossa, to watch as 'the whole rotten structure [comes] crashing down'. The German thrust that finally came to an exhausted halt on 5 December was, in places, actually east of Moscow.

MOSCOW COUNTERATTACK

The tanks of General Guderian's 2nd Panzer Army were at Mikhaylov, about 150km (93 miles) south and 30km (19 miles) east of the Soviet capital. To the north of the city, the tanks of General Erich Höppner's 4th Panzer Group had reached the tram stops of Moscow's outer suburbs before they were halted by the 20th and 33rd Armies of the Soviet Western Front. On 8 December, as winter set in, the German commanders realised that they must go onto the defensive.

The warnings of the Soviet agent Richard Sorge about Barbarossa may have been ignored, but his most important information for Stalin was that the Japanese did not intend to capitalise on the Soviet Union's misfortunes in 1941 and invade from Manchuria. This allowed the Stavka (Soviet High Command) to move their high-quality Siberian troops from the east and employ them in the counterattack at Moscow in the winter of 1941–42.

LEFT: A German light-gun crew in a village in western Russia in 1941. They have heavy-duty harness straps over their shoulders to assist in manhandling the gun.

FAR LEFT: The shattered, burning remains of a German aircraft shot down by Soviet anti-aircraft (AA) fire in the winter of 1941.

Tall, untidy and a heavy drinker, Sorge became something of a character in the German community in Japan, living in a flat in a slum district of Tokyo. He and his Japanese assistant were finally arrested in October 1941. Reports say that he was hanged in Tokyo on 7 November 1944.

On 6 December, the Red Army, under General Georgi Zhukov, who had already galvanised the defences of Leningrad, launched the counterattack at Moscow.

The Soviet counterattack was ambitious, with attacks carried out along a wide front by the North-Western Front, Kalinin Front, Western Front and South-Western Front forces between 18 and 22 January 1942. There was even an airborne landing by the 21st Parachute Brigade and 250th Airborne Regiment to the rear of the forces of German Army Group Centre facing Moscow.

STAND AND FIGHT

The fighting lasted from December 1941 to March 1942 and, in that time, the German forces pulled back in some sectors as much as 500km (310 miles). Hitler sacked the Army Commander in Chief, Field Marshal von Brauchitsch, took command of the German Army, and ordered it to stand and fight. Two pockets to the north at Demyansk and Kholm held out, were supplied by air, and were later relieved by the 16th Army. On 19 December 1941, Hitler had issued a General Order that included the words: 'Every man must fight where he stands. No falling back where there are no prepared positions in the rear.' The successful defence of these small pockets and the 'stand and fight' order that actually prevented the collapse of Army Group Centre would be seen by Hitler as a panacea for all subsequent battles of encirclement, notably that of the 6th Army at Stalingrad a year later.

With the onset of the spring mud, the front finally stabilised. German soldiers who survived this harsh period received the *Ostmedaille* (Eastern Medal). In the *Landsers'* grim slang, this eastern campaign medal was known as the *Gefrierfleischorden* – the 'Cold Meat' Medal or, more kindly, the 'Frost' Medal.

Writing in the army newspaper *Red Star*, the Russian writer and propagandist Ilya Ehrenburg commented dryly on the German Army's experience of the winter of 1941–42: 'The Russian winter was a surprise for the Prussian tourists.'

LEFT: The Mozjayskoye Shosse boulevard in Moscow prepared for street fighting in October 1941. The civilian population was mobilised to construct defences both around and in the city. A narrow access has been left for vehicles on the left of the barricade that consists of hedgehog anti-tank obstacles, with a sand-bagged parapet to protect the infantry. If the infantry behind the sand bags were not in a position to fire on the obstacles, enemy engineers could move forwards and demolish them.

RIGHT: Red Navy naval infantry on Mount Mitridat in the Kerch Peninsula in the Crimea in 1941. With ships sunk or trapped, sailors were used as infantry in Leningrad, Sevastopol and, later, Stalingrad. In the fighting at Sevastopol, the naval infantry wore a distinctive fouled anchor insignia. To preserve their naval identity, they often wore their caps and blue-and-white striped vests. These sailors wear Maxim machine-gun belts, probably as a way of carrying spare ammunition.

RIGHT: Supply troops of the German 11th Army on a muddy road in the Crimea in November 1941. The naval base of Sevastopol would not fall until 3 July 1942, after a long siege. Although the German Army was presented to the world as armoured and mechanised, much of it still relied on horse-drawn transport to pull guns and supply wagons. The Panzer Grenadiers might have ridden in the SdKfz 251 half-tracks, but most of the infantry in Russia marched eastwards in leather boots.

LEFT: Drivers of a German supply unit urge their horses up a hill through a town in the western Soviet Union. To survive in the harsh Russian winters, the ideal horses for transport units to use were those that were locally bred. The big German Army wagons that had been fine on the roads of Western Europe were also discarded by many units in favour of the little Russian one-horse *panje* wagons.

RIGHT: A *panje* wagon laden with hay pulls off to the side of a muddy road in a Russian village to allow German Army wagons to move through on 27 November 1941. The contrast in size between the Russian vehicles – which, although small, were light and manoeuvrable – and the big German ones, with their teams of horses, can be seen. Autumn rains, poor road surfaces and tracked, wheeled and horse-drawn transport quickly turned roads into almost impassable mud baths.

ABOVE: The cooks of a Red Army field kitchen ladle out a hot meal to troops near Kharkov in the winter of 1941. The city fell to the German 6th Army after a stiff fight in early November 1941. The food being served in the field kitchen is probably *kasha*, a filling buckwheat porridge that could be flavoured with vegetables or meat as available. The soldiers are wearing steel helmets, but have felt caps underneath to protect their heads from heat loss.

LEFT: A section of Soviet soldiers advance in early winter covered by a Pulemet Degtyareva Pekhotnii (DP) light machine-gun crew. The men have not yet been issued with white camouflage smocks and so stand out against the snow. The Soviet soldiers who were assigned to Punishment Battalions did not receive this type of camouflage clothing, as it was reported that one of their frontline functions was to draw enemy fire so that their weapons and positions could be identified and located, respectively.

ABOVE: Senior Lieutenant V. S. Efremov of the 10th Guards Bomber Regiment stands on the wing of his Ilyushin DB-3BF long-range bomber as the two 820kW (1100hp) M-88B engines are run up. Although the bomber served from 1941 to 1944, the officer's uniform suggests that the picture was taken in the winter in 1941. The DB-3BF bombers did attack the Reich in 1941, but they were soon forced eastwards to airfields that put them out of range of these lucrative targets. They also suffered at the hands of the rampant German fighter pilots, many of whom became aces in the first few months of the campaign in the Soviet Union.

LEFT: With their *shashka* (straight-bladed sabres) drawn, Soviet cavalry charge a village in the winter of 1941. While some German soldiers had encountered Polish cavalry in 1939, the numbers and aggression of the Soviet cavalry came as a shock to all who were on the receiving end of an attack. The most vulnerable were logistic troops behind the lines, who lacked the protection of large numbers of armed infantry and tanks. One German soldier, recalling an attack, felt that death delivered by a sabre-wielding horseman seemed almost archaic to members of the Wehrmacht.

ABOVE: PzKpfw III tanks grind through a Russian town in early winter in 1941. The German Army was ill prepared for the perishing cold of Russia and the shock of the first winter of the war in the East was considerable. By 1942, tanks had been equipped with special track extensions to enable them to operate in deep snow and reversible two-piece winter uniforms and felt and leather boots had been produced for the men. These items did not, however, reach the 6th Army at Stalingrad.

BELOW: A PzKpfw IV tank takes a position covered by a farm building and observes as two tanks of the troop move forwards. The potential threat from Soviet guns or tanks cannot be high, as the commanders are sitting high in their hatches and the gunner and radio operator in the tank in the middle distance are also leaning out of the turret hatches. Winter comes quickly in central Russia and these tanks have not yet received their whitewash camouflage.

ABOVE: A column of the Romanian Mountain Rifles (*Vânatori de Munte*) of the 10th Mountain Corps, with pack horses, moves towards Sevastopol on 11 December 1941. Under the overall command of Lieutenant General von Manstein, the Romanian troops performed well, as the Germans were aware of and took into account their limitations in equipment, training and leadership. The siege of Odessa earlier in the year, largely conducted by Romanian forces, had drawn off many Soviet soldiers who could have been used more effectively defending the port of Sevastopol.

RIGHT: A German sZgkw 12-tonne Typ DB 10, SdKfz 8 heavy half-track tows a 15cm (5.9in) sFH 18 gun through the mud and snow. The vehicle had originally been intended for export to the Soviet Union in the early 1930s, but, following Hitler's seizure of power in 1933, this deal was cancelled. The half-track could tow a load of 14 tonnes and the crew of an artillery piece were able to ride on the bench seats on the vehicle. Between 1939 and 1944, some 4000 of these half-tracks were built by Krupp, Krauss-Maffei and Skoda.

ABOVE: The bakers and staff of a German infantry division field bakery display a sign proudly boasting their production of 2,000,000 loaves in December 1941. Flour was readily available from the huge mills and granaries of the collective farms of the western Soviet Union – particularly the Ukraine, where the Germans were welcomed as liberators. Although rations were forwarded to German troops on the Eastern Front, they were also able to live off the land and, in occupied areas, the local population suffered as produce, raw materials and four million slave labourers were shipped back to the Third Reich.

LEFT: A captured Soviet *Sredny Tank T-34* (medium tank T-34) M1941 guards a road through a village, as a snow-camouflaged Renault ADK 4x2 light truck drives past on 17 December 1941. The German Army in the Soviet Union used a huge variety of vehicles that had been captured in Europe between 1939 and 1941 both to fight and to transport materials. However, this posed major logistics and spare parts problems. In Russia, they also used captured T-34 tanks, which, although basic, were reliable, particularly in the local conditions, and had excellent cross-country performance.

ABOVE: Soldiers of the Spanish *Division Azul* (Blue Division), so named because of the blue shirts of the Falangist uniform that its members wore when it was first deployed to Russia. Commanded by General Munoz Grandes, the *Division Azul* was made up of volunteers from Franco's Spain and fought in the Soviet Union from October 1941 until spring 1944. It is estimated that, of the 47,000 Spaniards who served in the division, 22,000 became casualties, of whom 4500 in turn were killed or died. Only 300 Spanish prisoners were repatriated from the Soviet Union in 1954.

LEFT: A German convoy during the fighting withdrawal in Russia on 2 January 1942. The OKW planners had not considered the possibility of a winter campaign and so soldiers were woefully ill equipped to cope with the conditions. The men in this photograph have used bed linen to improvise a winter camouflage cover over their greatcoats. The covers to their helmets have been secured in place with loops of tyre inner tube. For the men in the exposed open-top vehicle, wind chill would be an added misery.

RED STAR AT SEA

The Soviet Navy fought on land, as well as at sea. Sailors without ships proved very effective naval infantry, fighting at Sevastopol, Stalingrad and Leningrad.

BELOW: One of the 21 destroyers of the Soviet Black Sea Fleet turns to starboard to begin an attack on an enemy submarine. The Germans deployed six U-boats to the Black Sea, while the Romanians had three. After the Luftwaffe sank three destroyers, Stalin forbade the Black Sea Fleet from committing its major vessels – an old battleship and six cruisers – to operations against Axis forces. The fleet was subsequently used during the war to evacuate troops and also launched several amphibious landings.

RIGHT: According to the original caption, the crew of this Black Sea fleet submarine commanded by Captain Ivanov is preparing to engage an aircraft during the fighting at Sevastopol in 1942. In reality, faced by the prospect of an air attack, a submarine captain would probably give the order to dive, since the boat would be very vulnerable to cannon and machine-gun fire, as well as damage from bombs or depth charges, if it remained on the surface. It would also not be able to outrun its attacker on the surface.

ABOVE: Red Navy naval infantry or *Morskaia Pekhota* raise their banner on Mount Mitridat in the Kerch peninsula in the Crimea in 1941. The Kerch peninsula at the eastern end of the Crimea was the site of 25 separate landings, in ten different areas, on the night of 25/26 December 1941 – however only four of these succeeded and were reinforced. The Germans were forced back out of the Kerch peninsula, but returned later in 1942 to recapture it.

LEFT: Torpedo boats, part of the 84 boats in the Black Sea Fleet on patrol on 23 February 1942. Constructed of plywood and powered by aircraft engines, they were extremely fast, but also very vulnerable. Veterans recalled that a hit from even small-calibre guns could result in the destruction of the boat and loss of its crew. The torpedo boats of the Black Sea Fleet failed to intercept German and Romanian ships during Axis evacuation operations later in the war when the tide had turned.

ABOVE: Men of the Romanian Mountain Rifles (*Vânatori de Munte*) on the march in Crimea on 3 January 1942. They wear their distinctive khaki beret adopted from the French Army. Romanian troops who had fought in the Crimea were entitled to wear the German campaign decoration, the *Krimschild* (Crimea Shield), a bronze shield-shaped metal badge.

RIGHT: A column of German soldiers on the march on 6 January 1942.

LEFT: A German MG34 machine-gun crew brings the gun into action on its sustained fire tripod mount in a village in Russia on 3 February 1942. The MG34 was the weapon with which the German forces entered the war. It weighed 11.9kg (26.2lbs) in the light role and 31.07kg (68.5lbs) on the buffered sustained-fire mount that gave it sufficient stability to reach out to a maximum range of 2000m (2187yds).

ABOVE: Whitewashed T-34/76B tanks of a Yakunin's unit move through the town of Izyum, near Kharkov, in January 1942. The unit's political officer has arranged for a patriotic slogan to be painted on the turret. Patriotism and the defence of Mother Russia were more appealing than Communist exhortations.

BELOW: A young German MG34 machine gunner and his assistant smile, as others plod grimly through the snow. The men's heads are poorly protected against the cold by the M1938 *Feldmütze* cap – later versions had flaps that could be unbuttoned to fold down around the wearer's ears.

LEFT: Soviet trucks move across the Ice Road over the frozen Lake Ladoga during the siege of Leningrad. The German and Finnish forces failed to completely surround the city, and, during the winters of 1941–42 and 1942–43, food and ammunition were moved across the lake and casualties evacuated. A more comprehensive evacuation programme was not undertaken, however, because the city's Communist Party chief, Andrei Zhdanov, feared that Stalin would regard such a move as defeatist.

BELOW: Delivery of food to the frontline position of one of the subunits of the 21st Army of the Soviet South-Western Front in January 1942.

BELOW: Armoured troop-carrying sledges powered by aircraft engines employed by the Soviet 11th Army in their attack across Lake Ilmen on the night of 7/8 January 1942 against the German logistics centre at Staraya Russa. Although these vehicles had been used in the Winter War of 1939-40 against the Finns, they still came as a considerable surprise to the Germans. After some very tough fighting, the Germans were able to hold the line against the novel attack.

RIGHT: Stooping low, Soviet infantry move along a trench in the winter of 1941–42. Their white camouflage suits would conceal them very effectively in the snow, but movement would be obvious against the background. The trench has been dug with the bulk of the dug-up soil, or spoil, thrown forwards towards the enemy, on the right of the picture. The rule of thumb was two spadeloads of spoil towards the enemy, and one to the rear.

BELOW: The German MG34 machine gunner uses the optical sight on the MG-Lafatte 34 sustained-fire mount as he fires the gun using the grip trigger that has a mechanical linkage to the trigger on the gun. The empty, 50-round metal ammunition belt can be seen hanging from the right-hand side of the gun. This could be reloaded when the crew had withdrawn from the line and linked together and carried as 250 rounds in an ammunition box.

RIGHT: German horse-drawn supply vehicles move past a blazing apartment block in a Russian town on 26 February 1942. The extreme cold and sharp frosts of midwinter had made the muddy roads viable. However, for survival, it was critical to be under cover during the night. The block has probably been set on fire by the withdrawing German forces to ensure that it could not be used by Soviet troops for accommodation.

LEFT: Soviet soldiers captured on 1 February 1942, in the bitter fighting in Feodosiya in the Crimea, are assembled prior to evacuation to the rear. They are dressed in greatcoats and wear the *shapka-ushanka,* the synthetic fur pile or felt, ear-flapped cap introduced in 1940. One man has retained his M1938 lightweight pack. Soviet troops had landed at Feodosiya on 28 December 1941, and cut off the Kerch peninsula in the east of the Crimea, delaying the attack on Sevastopol.

RIGHT: A Tupolev SB-2bis bomber of the South-Western Front runs up its engines before a night mission in March 1942. The bomber, powered by two 619kW (830hp) M-100 engines, had a maximum speed of 410km/h (255mph) at 4000m (13,123ft), and a range of 1200km (746 miles). It had a crew of three and the defensive armament of two nose-mounted 7.62mm (0.3in) ShKAS machine guns, one in a dorsal hatch and one in a ventral position.

RIGHT: Soviet scouts P. C. Borenov (left) and S. I. Bolotkin of the South-Western Front, on a reconnaissance patrol in March 1942. Dogs were widely used in the Soviet Army for carrying messages, retrieving wounded, detecting mines and, with explosives strapped to their backs, even as anti-tank mines. In this last role, they were trained to run under tanks, where the belly armour would depress the trigger mechanism attached to the charge. The dogs in this picture are probably trained to smell or hear the enemy.

BELOW: Soldiers of the 21st Army of the South-Western Front, assisted by civilians from the town of Shebekino in the Kursk region, construct a bridge across the Nezjegol River in March 1942. Both sides used civilian men and women to assist in the construction of defences and roads and bridges. While the ground is frozen hard and the snows have not melted and filled up the rivers, this work would have been undertaken with some urgency so that it could be completed before the river turned into a torrent with the coming of spring. To the left of the picture appears to be the charred remains of the former bridge across the Nezjegol, burnt by the Germans during their retreat.

ABOVE: A Soviet triple AA machine-gun crew of the Kalinin Front scan the skies in April 1942. The ammunition boxes on the mount are positioned forwards of the guns to ensure that the centre of balance makes the guns easier to traverse. Normally, the belted ammunition would feed in from the right. The circular AA sight enables the gunner to calculate the lead he must give to an aircraft flying across his line of fire; the tracer rounds in the belt would also assist in visually adjusting aim.

LEFT: A Beriev MBR-2bis short-range maritime reconnaissance flying boat piloted by Senior Lieutenant T. Kuznetsov takes off from the Black Sea in April 1942. More than 1500 Berievs were built between 1934 and 1941. The flying boat had a crew of four or five, and could carry 300kg (661lbs) of bombs, depth charges or mines. Although production ceased during the war, the Beriev was in continued use long after 1945, in roles such as fishery protection and as a passenger aircraft with eight seats.

BELOW: The 30m (98ft) long barrel of the German 80cm (31.5in) long-range rail gun K(E) 'Gustav' that was employed in the siege of Sevastopol. It took 1500 men a month to assemble the gun, which weighed 135 tonnes in action, and to prepare the two strengthened parallel railway tracks to take the huge piece. Gustav, also known as 'Dora', fired a 4800kg (10,582lb) shell to a maximum range of 47km (29.2 miles). Its main function was to destroy the forts and coastal batteries around Sevastopol.

ABOVE: Some of the few civilians who were evacuated from Leningrad make their way eastwards across the 352km (220-mile) Ice Road over Lake Ladoga on 12 April 1942. The thaw is setting in in this photograph, as the trucks are driving through water. The road finally closed on 15 April 1942 and, on that day, 3000 people died in Leningrad. A year later, in January 1943, the Soviet Army managed to establish a rail link to the city, although Leningrad was still largely surrounded and under German fire.

ABOVE: Combat engineers of the 526th Sapper Battalion of the 21st Army of the South-Western Front, cutting a barbed-wire fence near the village of Alekseevka in Kursk district, in April 1942. As two men cut the wire, a third stands by as a protection party. An operation as hazardous as this would probably be conducted at night and, judging by the position of the photographer, the sappers were probably in training or practising before going out into the short spring night.

CHAPTER FOUR

Stalingrad

Enemy at the Gates

On 8 May 1942, the Germans launched their new offensive, *Unternehmen Blau* (Operation Blue). In savage fighting at Kharkov between 12 and 28 May, they defeated a Soviet offensive and then rolled eastwards. After a long siege, the Black Sea naval base of Sevastopol fell on 2 July. Following exceptionally fierce street fighting, in which artillery was used at point-blank ranges, Rostov, on the River Don, fell on 23 July.

On the same day, Hitler instructed Army Group North to prepare for the capture of Leningrad by early September. The operation was originally code-named *Feuerzauber* (Fire Magic) and then renamed *Nordlicht* (Northern Light). Despite a series of massive assaults, the city held.

In the heat of 24 August, the 6th Army, part of Army Group A under List, reached Stalingrad on the Volga. For many of the Ukrainians and Don Cossacks, the German forces were greeted as liberators from Stalin's repressive government. To the south, the summer offensive extended to its furthest limits on 18 November. It reached the burning oil wells of Maikop on 9 August and then into the Caucasus and within 113km (70 miles) of Grozny.

In 1942, the map of Europe and North Africa was coloured red as either an ally or a conquest of the Third Reich, the only exceptions being Sweden, Spain, Portugal, Switzerland and, of course, Britain. Secret contacts had even been made by the Soviet Union with Germany to explore the possibility of calling a ceasefire, to be followed by peace negotiations. Stalin was on record as saying, 'In war I would deal with the Devil and his grandmother.'

Germany's dominance was a powerful and beguiling image, but one which was soon to change. As the 6th Army

LEFT: Cossack cavalry of the South-Western Front breast a rise as they attack German positions in April 1942. After 1941, Soviet cavalry units were grouped in corps, composed of three divisions. A division had about 5040 men and 5128 horses, with minimal logisitical back-up.

FAR LEFT: A Soviet sniper wrapped in a captured German camouflage tent-half in the summer of 1942.

pushed into the factories and railway yards of Stalingrad, the German forces lost the advantage of mobility and firepower, and became bogged down in grinding streetfighting. Territorial gains were measured in streets, buildings and even rooms. The capture of Stalingrad would give the Germans control of the Volga, access to Astrakhan and the supply of petroleum from the south.

TOUGH COMMANDER

Stalingrad was held by a tough and ruthless Soviet commander, General Vasili Chuikov, but, by 18 November 1942, the men of his 62nd Army had only toeholds on the west bank, including the huge Tractor, Barrikady and Krasny Oktyabr factories. The Soviets had been bombed and shelled, and discipline imposed to keep them in the front line by the *Narodnyy Kommissariat Vnutrennikh Del* (the NKVD, or People's Commissariat for Domestic Affairs) secret police units had been ruthless. The best of the German forces were now entangled in Stalingrad and, on their northern flank on the River Don bend, the front lines were held by less well-equipped and trained Romanian and Italian troops. Due to poor administration, however, the 6th Army did not receive cold-weather uniforms with the onset of winter.

ABOVE: With one man on guard, the 76mm (3in) gun crew of Sergeant Sydorjevskiy, part of the Artillery Regiment of the 21st Soviet Army of the South-Western Front, breaks for lunch in Alexeevka in the Kursk district in April 1942. Captured German mess tins were much preferred by the Soviet soldiers to their own aluminium pots.

On 19 November, Zhukov launched Operation Uranus. He positioned the South-West Front – consisting of the 63rd Army, 1st Guards Army and 21st Army, a total of one million men, 13,500 guns and 894 tanks – opposite the Romanian 3rd Army and Italian 8th Army. The Soviets tanks and infantry tore through the Axis forces. In five days, they linked up with men of the 51st Army south of Stalingrad and closed the trap.

Hitler insisted that the 6th Army make no attempt to break out from Stalingrad. Field Marshal Herman Göring, head of the Luftwaffe, assured Hitler that it could supply the trapped army, a promise beyond its capability. The lumbering Ju 52 transports did manage to fly out some casualties and bring in supplies, but intense anti-aircraft fire and long flights made it an increasingly hazardous journey. On the ground, Field Marshal von Manstein, commanding the 4th Panzer Army, was ordered to break into the encirclement and attempted this between 12 and 23 December. If the 6th Army had been allowed to break out to meet him, they might have saved many lives. The Russians halted the relief attempt and kept up pressure on the pocket. Day by day, they closed in on the working airfields and finally had them within artillery range.

On Christmas Day, the Propaganda Ministry broadcast greetings from the crew of a U-boat in the Atlantic, men of the *Afrika* Corps in North Africa, the garrison of the Atlantic Wall and, over a crackling radio link, the men of Stalingrad, 'the front on the Volga'. Their voices then blended together in '*Stille Nacht*', the classic German Christmas carol. It was dramatic and very moving – and faked in radio studios in Berlin.

On 31 January 1943, the recently-promoted Field Marshal Paulus surrendered. At a luncheon conference in Germany, Hitler snapped, 'The duty of the men at Stalingrad is to be dead'; many had fulfilled his orders. Figures for the Russian victory at Stalingrad are hard to establish, but German and Axis losses were in the region of one and a half million men, 3500 tanks, 12,000 guns and mortars, 75,000 vehicles and 3000 aircraft.

In Moscow in the winter of 1941–42, Nazi Germany was fated not to win World War II; at Stalingrad a year later, it was doomed to lose it. The year 1942 was a significant one, not only for the victory at Stalingrad. It was also the year that Soviet war production overtook that of Germany: 24,000 to 4800 in armoured vehicles and 21,700 to 14,700 in aircraft.

RIGHT: Smoke rises from a village in the Poltava region in 1942. The smoke's colour and intensity suggests that German bombers have hit either fuel dumps or vehicle concentrations. In the first two years of the war, the Luftwaffe had the numerical, qualitative and tactical advantage over the Red Air Force and could attack targets behind Russian lines. By 1943, this edge was rapidly shifting in favour of Soviet forces and their fighter pilots - both men and women were becoming aces against Hitler's Luftwaffe.

ABOVE: A seaman of the Black Sea Fleet stands guard over a camouflaged coastal gun in the Crimea. The 12 batteries protecting Sevastopol from attack were the responsibility of the Soviet Navy and comprised 42 guns, ranging from 152mm (6in) to 305mm (12in) in calibre, in armoured turrets and concrete emplacements. The largest battery was Maxim Gorky to the north, but others, such as Fort Balaclava and Maxim Gorky II covered the southern coast. Some forts bore less congenial or historic names such as 'Cheka' and 'GRU' (the latter being the acronym for the Soviet secret police).

ABOVE: Cossack cavalry at the charge in the Crimea in 1942. The men wear the traditional black astrakhan caps or *papacha*, and have drawn their *shashka* (traditional straight-bladed sabres). Cossacks do not traditionally wear spurs and use instead a whip and a *nagaika*, the distinctive wooden-framed saddle with its leather cushion which gave them a characteristic high seat. Although they were used in massed attacks, Cossack troops were ideal for reconnaissance and patrols in difficult terrain such as mountains or marshland.

BELOW: A column of Soviet prisoners of war marches westwards from Kerch on 15 May 1942. The men are part of the Crimea Front, commanded by Major General D. T. Kozlov, which was attacked by German and Romanian forces under Lieutenant General von Manstein in May 1942. Although outnumbered, the Axis forces used an amphibious landing on 8 May 1942 to unhinge the Soviet defences and, after 10 days' fighting, they were broken by the German attackers. The Crimean Front lost more than 170,000 men as prisoners.

ABOVE: Soviet soldiers from the South-Western Front move through a village near Kharkov in the eastern Ukraine, supported by a GAZ BA-32 6 x 4 armoured car. The BA-32 had a crew of four and was armed with one 45mm (1.77in) gun and two 7.62mm (0.3in) machine guns. The armoured car was based on the chassis of the 1.5-tonne GAZ-AAA truck, a vehicle that was also used for the Katyusha 16 rail surface-to-surface rocket launchers and quad-mounted Maxim AA machine guns.

RIGHT: Engineers from a platoon commanded by Senior Lieutenant Voronko sprint across an infantry pontoon bridge that has been damaged by German artillery fire in the summer of 1942. This small river is not a major obstacle when compared to some of the huge rivers in Russia which are so wide that only long-range artillery could hit positions on the far bank. Gunners would register river banks as targets for fire missions because enemy troops would concentrate there before crossing.

RIGHT: The battleship *Sevastopol* firing its main armament in a ship-to-shore bombardment of targets near the town of Sudak in the Crimea in 1942. The Soviet Navy had three battleships, but the force had been neglected for nearly 20 years following the Revolution, and had been seen as having a purely defensive role. In 1938, a programme of building and modernisation was begun, but the German invasion in 1941 halted this work and, during the war, efforts were concentrated on patrol boats and submarines.

ABOVE: Burned and blasted Red Army vehicles of the South Front caught by Luftwaffe bombers as they waited to attempt a crossing of the River Don by ferry on 15 July 1942. Choke points such as ferries, bridges and gorges were obvious targets for air attacks. This attack was part of *Unternehmen Blau* (Operation Blue), the German ground and air attack that was launched by Army Group A and Army Group B driving southwestwards towards the Caucasus on 8 May 1942.

ABOVE: Red Air Force Ilyushin DB-3F bombers in 1942. Some 6800 of these bombers were produced between 1937 and 1944. They were the first Soviet aircraft to bomb Berlin when the 332 Special Purposes Heavy Bomber Regiment attacked the German capital on 8/9 August 1941. The maximum internal and external bomb load was 2500kg (5511lbs) and the aircraft had a crew of three.

RIGHT: A group of officers from the headquarters of the 632nd Infantry Regiment of the 175th Infantry Division, at a command post near the village of Tarasovka in the Kiev-Syvatoshino district on 27 August 1942. In the centre at the rear is Major B. A. Ulianovsky, Chief of Staff of the 632nd Regiment. The men are not expecting an imminent attack, as they have all in a relaxed pose; but they are still wearing their helmets.

ABOVE: Soviet soldiers take cover as a shell explodes at night during a patrol in the Kerch Peninsula in the Crimea in August 1942. Blast and shell fragments from a shell burst normally go upwards in a lobe-shaped cone and so lying prone reduces the risk of death or injury from the blast or shrapnel. A sustained heavy bombardment, however, can stun soldiers into disarray and destroy their positions and equipment. By the end of the war, the Soviet Army had become masters of heavy artillery bombardments and were able to pound German positions to pieces before an attack.

RIGHT: Troops commanded by S. A. Dubinchik advance under fire in the Kerch area of the Crimea in August 1942. The regular spacing of the simultaneous bursts suggests that like many 'action' photographs taken in World War II, this was in fact a staged picture. Although some photographers and film cameramen strove for authenticity, for others it was safer to 'stunt' a picture. This had the added benefit of ensuring that it was a well-composed, correctly focused, good-quality image.

ABOVE: Soviet soldiers of the South-Western Front in a localised counterattack during the German advance in the area of Kharkov in the summer of 1942. All the men are armed with the ubiquitous PPSh-41 submachine gun and are wearing the basic kit of a Soviet soldier, including a greatcoat or blanket with haversack, entrenching tool and a rolled groundsheet. The coat or blanket would be used as a covering during sleep. Although this is a dramatic shot, it is once again likely that this photograph has been posed, as the photographer would otherwise have been in a very exposed position.

LEFT: A 152mm (6in) M1937 howitzer crew load their weapon prior to engaging targets near the town of Zaporozhzhye in August 1942. The howitzer weighed 7128kg (15,715lbs) in action and fired a 43.6kg (96lb) shell to a maximum range of 17.3km (10.7 miles). A trained crew could keep up a rate of fire of four rounds a minute. The gun's trail added significantly to the weapon's weight. From 1944 onwards, the Soviets also mounted the gun on the massive JSU-152 heavy assault gun, which was used against tanks and reinforced concrete bunkers and emplacements.

ABOVE: The Kuban Cossacks of Lieutenant General Kirichenko's 17th Cavalry Corps who, at the end of August 1942, were promoted to Guards status, as the 4th Guards Cavalry Corps. As they ride through the North Caucasus in August 1942, they appear to be escorting the trucks of their motorised supply column. Although Cossack cavalry might find fodder and water for their horses locally, they still required rations, ammunition for themselves and blacksmithing and farrier support for their mounts. Nonetheless, compared to, say, an armoured division, the Cossacks travelled light and could move quickly.

RIGHT: Soldiers of the South-Western Front sit on a captured Sturmgeschütz III Ausf B bis D SdKgfz 142 assault gun. The vehicle had 50mm (1.97in) frontal and 30mm (1.2in) hull armour and a limited traverse, short 75mm (2.95in) StuK L/24 or L/33 gun, but initially no hull-mounted machine gun. In the F to G marks, this was rectified and frontal armour was increased to 70mm (2.75in). The StuG III B to D had a cross-country range of 90km (56 miles) and 140km (87 miles) on roads; in F to G marks, this was reduced to 80km (50 miles) and 130km (81 miles), respectively.

LEFT: Dressed in his chemical warfare clothing, a seaman of the Black Sea Fleet mans an anti-aircraft gun during a gas attack drill in 1942. The *schlem* respirator with its close-fitting rubber mask would remain virtually unchanged until the 1980s. This version would allow the wearer to hear orders, but, since it has no built-in voice box, the sailor would only be able to communicate by sign language once he was wearing his gas mask. Both the Soviets and the Germans had large stocks of chemical weapons, but they were not used, probably due to a fear of retaliation. Chemical weapons had been used by the Japanese in Manchuria in the late 1930s, though, so their use was certainly not unheard of, and gas masks were issued to most soldiers for the duration of the war.

RIGHT: Thick, black smoke pours from the funnels of a Red Navy cruiser in the Black Sea, as it frantically lays a smoke screen to cover a mine-laying operation in 1942. The cruiser was one of six in the fleet, a force initially commanded by Vice-Admiral F. S. Oktyabrsky. Following the loss of several destroyers to German air attack, however, Vice-Admiral Oktyabrsky was replaced on Stalin's orders and, from May 1943 to March 1944, the Black Sea Fleet was commanded by Vice-Admiral Lev Vladimirsky.

ABOVE: Trailing plumes of dust, a column of German tanks and trucks grinds forwards on a road stretching to the horizon near the River Don on 1 September 1942. The heat of the Russian summers and dust from the poor roads increased wear on the engines of armoured and soft-skinned vehicles, and caused mechanical failure and maintenance problems. The crews of vehicles would sometimes be left alone for days waiting for mechanics to arrive to repair their vehicle.

BELOW: The minesweeper *Mariupol* from the Azovsk Fleet. The Sea of Azov to the east of the Crimea was part of the Black Sea Fleet's area of responsibility; however, when German forces crossed the Kerch Strait onto the Taman Peninsula in September 1942, the inland sea was completely cut off. Surviving ships from the Black Sea Fleet, including cruisers, were forced to find shelter in ports in the southeast, close to the Turkish border.

LEFT: A motorcycle combination follows behind a detachment of Marder III *Panzerjäger* anti-tank guns in the advance towards Stalingrad in September 1942. The Marder III used captured Soviet 76.2mm (3in) FK 296 anti-tank guns, which had been taken in large numbers in 1941 – ironically, the Marder III was the only weapon capable of defeating tanks such as the Soviet T-34 and KV-1 and KV-2. The gun was mounted on a Czech 38 (t) tank chassis, and thus became an effective mobile tank killer.

ABOVE: The crew of a German PzKpfw IV tank of the XIV Panzer Corps observe the smoke rising from a distant action on the steppes to the west of Stalingrad on 3 September 1942. This followed the breakthrough of the defences of the Soviet 62nd Army by the Panzer Corps on 22 August 1942. The terrain seen in this photograph is ideal for armoured warfare, with little cover and good visibility – in the factories and sewers of Stalingrad, this advantage would disappear.

ABOVE: Two men of the 31st Army of the Stalingrad front, Privates Kokarev and Zionchenko, man a position during the fighting in the town of Serafimovich in September 1942. They are armed with a captured Italian Fucile Mitriagliatori Breda Modello 30, an air-cooled light machine gun that fired a 6.5mm (0.25in) round at between 450 and 500 rpm.

BELOW: Soldiers of the 21st Army of the Stalingrad Front, dressed against the autumn rain in their capes, listen to a morale-boosting speech from the head of the Political Department, Leonid I. Sokolov, in September 1942. Some of the soldiers are wearing the M1936 helmet with its distinctive flared brim and crest on the crown.

RIGHT: Tank riders of the Southern Front have dismounted from their T-34 steeds and advance against German positions in the Donbass Region in 1942. They are armed with the robust and very effective PPSh-41 submachine gun. This weapon used simple production techniques of stamping and brazing, weighed 3.56kg (7.84lbs) and had a 71-round drum or 35-round box magazine. It fired 900 rounds a minute.

LEFT: A triple Maxim machine gun AA mount on a truck is ferried by raft across the River Don, near Serafimovich, in September 1942.

BELOW: One of the apparently endless columns of Soviet PoWs taken by the 6th Army, pictured on 15 September 1942 marching westwards to a grim fate as slave labour or worse in the Third Reich. Stalin regarded soldiers who had surrendered as traitors.

ABOVE: An M1939 37mm (1.45in) light AA gun, on the destroyer *Soobrazitelniy* commanded by Petty Officer V. S. Tarasov, in action in the Black Sea on 15 October 1942. The gun was based on the Swedish Bofors design and fired a five-round clip which was loaded from the top. A good crew could keep up a rate of fire of 80 rounds a minute. The maximum horizontal range for the M1939 was 800m (875yds) and the vertical 6000m (6562yds); however, the effective range was 1400m (1531yds). The gun could fire both high-explosive and armour-piercing ammunition – the latter being useful when it was used on land against light armour.

LEFT: A heavy AA gun crew commanded by Chief Petty Officer N. I. Avramenko, aboard the battle cruiser *Krasniy Kavkaz,* one of six ships in this class in the Black Sea Fleet, in the autumn of 1942. The crew is standing by to engage Luftwaffe bombers preparing to attack the fleet. The Germans claimed that the fleet lost one cruiser during the war. Although the crew of this AA gun are wearing M1940 steel helmets and have BN respirators slung ready for use, unlike ratings in the Royal or US Navy, for example, they do not have anti-flash hoods to protect their faces from flash burns, a common hazard when a ship is hit.

ABOVE: The tank riders have moved forwards to close with the German positions. This was a common Soviet tactic that required the infantry to neutralise anti-tank positions before the tanks made the breakthrough. The grim reality was that German machine guns would often cut down the infantry before they reached their objectives. When tank support was not available, infantrymen were deliberately intoxicated with vodka and sent forwards cheering, with arms linked, against the German positions.

BELOW: Tank riders dismount from a rather overcrowded T-34 near the town of Communarsk in the Voroshilov district in 1942. The photograph is probably posed, since the number of soldiers on the tank is unrealistic and the tank appears to be halted. The men would have obscured the crew's vision and restricted the turret's operation. Normal practice was for men to ride on the rear deck or, later, the sides, holding grab rails that had been welded onto the turret. They would dismount as the tank went into the attack and flush out the German infantry.

ABOVE: The political officer on the left, wearing an astrakhan cap, uses a cigarette holder to mitigate the harsh Russian tobacco, as he watches a young officer of the 21st Army of the South-Western Front brief a patrol commander. The soldier on the extreme left is armed with a 7.62mm (0.3in) Pistolet-Pulemet Degtyareva o1940G, or PPD1940 submachine gun. This was a well-designed weapon that weighed 3.63kg (8lbs), had a 71-round drum magazine and a cyclic rate of fire of 800 rpm, and had been used in action in Finland in 1940. Although easy to manufacture, it was replaced by the PPSh-41 submachine gun.

RIGHT: Soviet soldiers examine a Czech Skoda 100mm (3.93in) Model 14/19, in service with the German Army as the 100mm leFH 14/19(t), captured in 1942. The howitzer weighed 1505kg (3318lbs) in action and fired a 14kg (30.8lb) shell to a maximum range of 9970m (10,903yds). The gun was also used by Italian forces and, since an Italian expeditionary force of three divisions served in the Soviet Union, this piece could have been part of an Italian battery. It was a reliable if rather old-fashioned weapon.

LEFT: German soldiers firing a 75mm (2.95in) leichte Gebirgs Infantriegeschutz 18. L/11.8 infantry gun at buildings on the outskirts of Stalingrad on 28 October 1942. The gun was 900mm (35.4in) long and had a 884mm (34.8in) barrel, weighed 400kg (881lbs) in action and fired 6 (13.2lb) and 5.45kg (12lb) shells to a maximum range of 3550m (3882yds). Infantry guns were designed to give infantry battalions their own organic artillery support, which allowed them to engage short-range targets. Later in the war, the German Army used captured Soviet 120mm (4.7in) mortars in favour of infantry guns.

RIGHT: Private Kalmikov loads a Soviet 76.2 mm (3in) Field Gun Model 1939 (76-39) with gun layer Private Ovchinnikov, commanded by Corporal Khubardiev, in Stalingrad in October 1942. The gun has been sited within a building that protects it from artillery or air attack.

LEFT: The *Krasniy Octiabr* (Red October) heavy engineering plant, gutted by air attacks by the Luftwaffe, seen on 11 October 1942. The factory complex was defended by the 13th Guards Division. Eventually, by mid-November 1942, the Germans held part of the Red October factory, with the Guards fighting from the cold furnaces of the metal works. Along with the Tractor and Barrikady factories to the north, the Red October position would be the key to the defence of Stalingrad, preventing the 6th Army under General Paulus from reaching the Volga.

BELOW: Captioned 'A moment of battle for Stalingrad 1942–43', this photograph looks suspiciously like a re-staging of the battle. No photographer would be able, or prepared, to take a picture of this quality in the middle of a major armoured attack. The T-34 M1943 tanks have very untypical large stars and markings on the turret, and do not have the standard spare fuel drums on the rear deck that would have been fitted to ensure that the impetus of the attack could be maintained. Also, since the attack appears to be taking place in the summer – the major tank actions were fought in the winter of 1942–43 – the picture appears additionally suspect.

LEFT: German infantry prepare to move a 75mm (2.95in) leichte Infantriegeschutz 18. L/11.8 gun forwards during fighting in the Stalingrad suburbs in October 1942. The gun, developed by Rheinmetall, was the first new artillery piece to become standard German issue after World War I. It originally had spoked wheels, but these were replaced by pneumatic tyres. An experienced crew could fire between four and six shells a minute. Unusually, the barrel was enclosed in a square slipper and, when loading, pivoted upwards while the breech block remained fixed – a similar system to that used for loading a shotgun.

LEFT: Watched by a Soviet Navy Senior Lieutenant who holds his party membership card, a Soviet sailor signs the forms that admits him into the Communist Party, in Stalingrad in 1942. A soldier acts as a witness to the ceremony, which had almost religious overtones. As the strong ideological character of the war in the Soviet Union became evident, membership of the Party increased.

BELOW: Near Stalingrad in November 1942, tree trunks are positioned by men of the Artillery Bombardment Regiment of the Soviet 21st Army of the South-Western Front to build the roof of a bunker. Once they were in position, the dug-out earth was packed down and then camouflaged with straw. A well-dug bunker could withstand even a direct hit from a 150mm (5.91in) shell.

RIGHT:. An armoured train built at a railway workshop in the industrial town of Voroshilovgrad brings its guns to bear in the winter of 1942. Armoured trains were widely used as mobile power bases in the Red and White Civil War after World War I and, in 1941–42, saw action in the defence of Moscow and in the Ukraine. They were, however, obsolete and a photographic story showing German combat engineers attacking an immobilised train was featured in the German propaganda magazine *Signal*. In the Russian Civil War (1917–22), where the threat did not include tanks or aircraft, and stocks of explosives for destruction of the track were often not readily available, armoured trains were a potent mobile symbol of invincibility as much as a weapon of war.

RIGHT: Dressed in their short sheepskin coats and shoulders slung with map cases, the Communist Committee of a Guards Cavalry division of the South-Western Front holds a meeting in the winter of 1942. The picture looks suspiciously posed as, tough as they were, soldiers in the Soviet Army would probably have found shelter, rather than sit in the snow for such a meeting. To complete the composition, the group includes a sniper dressed in a camouflage suit.

LEFT: A German officer moves forwards carefully through the ruins of a building in Stalingrad. His lack of steel helmet and personal equipment suggests that the photograph was not taken close to the front line. He may be a military sight-seer or conducting a visual reconnaissance of a Soviet position. However, his caution indicates the threat of snipers, a constant fear for soldiers on both sides in fighting in cities. Movement spotted by forward observers would also attract fire from mortars and artillery.

LEFT: One of the photographers who produced the images in this book, V. Udin, a photographer with the 21st Soviet Army newspaper, stands by an abandoned German 150mm (5.9in) sFH18 howitzer in the Stalingrad perimeter in 1943. Udin's camera appears to be a German Leica, a tough, reliable camera that was probably captured or bought before the war. Watches and cameras were always desirable loot for Soviet soldiers and recently captured German prisoners would find themselves being asked for 'Photo?' – their cameras. The ready availability of cameras and the German tendency to photograph the worst sights on the Eastern Front, including mass executions, has left a permanent record of the atrocities committed in the Soviet Union.

LEFT: As an officer confirms orders on a field telephone, two soldiers of the Soviet 21st Army of the South-Western Front study a map of the area near Kalach-na-Donu west of Stalingrad in the winter of November/December 1942. The man on the left has armed himself with a captured German MP38/40 submachine gun. When the 21st Army captured the bridge at Kalach, they severed the German 6th Army's communications and, on 23 November, linked up with the 51st Army to surround the German forces.

RIGHT: The crew bring a German 88mm (3.45in) Flak 18/36 anti-aircraft gun into action at Stalingrad on 4 November 1942. The '88' fired a 9.4kg (20.7lb) shell and was deployed both as an anti-aircraft gun with an effective range of 8000m (8749yds) and anti-tank gun with a range of 14,813m (16,200yds). High-explosive shells had a muzzle velocity of 820m/s (2690ft/s) and the armour-piercing 795m/s (2608ft/s). A seasoned crew could fire at a rate of 15 rounds a minute, if the gun was fully manned and ammunition prepared in advance.

RIGHT: A soldier of the Soviet 62nd Army takes aim in what is possibly the remains of the blast furnaces of the Red October heavy engineering plant in central Stalingrad, in the early winter of 1942. In the foreground of the picture is coiled barbed wire that has been brought forwards and dumped so that, at night, the defenders can stretch it across gaps in the ruined walls to create new obstacles for the infantry of Germany's 6th Army. The photographer's position – behind cover – suggests that this photograph is not staged.

BELOW: Dragging a Maxim machine gun on its Sokolov mounting, soldiers of the 21st Army of the South-Western Front follow behind a T-70 light tank during fighting near the Kalatch bridge across the River Don in November 1942. The link-up between the 26th Tank Corps of the 21st Army and the 4th Tank Corps of the Stalingrad Front at Kalatch sealed the fate of the 6th Army. Although smoke is billowing in the picture, the soldiers' lack of urgency and the presence of a vehicle and observers on the bridge in the background indicate that this is a posed reconstruction.

ABOVE: A disconsolate group of German prisoners are marched to the rear by PPSh-41–armed guards of the Kalinin Front in 1942. Some of the prisoners wear the reversible two-piece winter uniform issued for the winter of 1942–43, garments that failed to reach the 6th Army at Stalingrad before they were cut off by Operation Uranus. The hooded quilted uniform was white on one side and either grey or camouflaged on the reverse. A button on the sleeve allowed the wearer to attach a coloured armband, in order to allow German soldiers to identify white-clad friend or foe.

LEFT: The crew of a T34/76D with soldiers of the 21st Army of the South-Western Front huddle on the tank's turrets during fighting near Stalingrad in Operation Uranus. The 21st Army, part of the South Western Front under General Nikolai Vatutin, initially had a hard fight with the 3rd Romanian Army on the northern Don, but punched through and swung south behind 6th Army. The T-34, with its wide tracks, could move across snow at speed, allowing armoured crews to use *Blitzkrieg*-style tactics of fast, deep penetration.

RIGHT: With his PPSh-41 submachine gun within easy reach, a signaller with the Soviet 62nd Army mans a field telephone in a basement command post on the west bank of the Volga in Stalingrad. By 18 November 1942, the 62nd Army had been forced back by the 6th Army's tanks and infantry to a toehold in Stalingrad. The longer the Soviet forces could hang on in Stalingrad, the greater the chance of success for Operation Uranus, the major Soviet counteroffensive launched on 19 November 1942.

BELOW: Commanders of the 26th Tank Corps of the South-Western Front with a map, discussing the situation with Major General A. G. Rodin in November 1942.

LEFT: A Soviet 120-HM 38 120mm (4.7in) mortar crew of the 32nd Army near Stalingrad await the order to fire, which appears to be by a rudimentary system of hand signals. The Germans were very impressed by the 6000m (6562yd) range and 16kg (35lb) weight of the high-explosive bomb of the 120-HM 38. They not only took captured mortars into service as the 120mm (4.7in) Granatwerfer 378 (r), but also manufactured their own improved copy as the 120mm (4.7in) Granatwerfer 42. This fired a 15.8kg (34.8lb) bomb out to 6025m (6589yds).

BELOW: An officer with a group of cheerful soldiers of the 62nd Army near Stalingrad. At first sight, they appear identical, in their greatcoats and *shapka-ushanka* caps. However, the soldiers' coats were secured with hooks, whereas officers' had buttons. The officer second from the right is also distinguished by his *Kozhanoe Snaryazhenie*, the brown leather 'Sam Brown' belt with five-pointed star buckle. The British provided greatcoats as part of their aid to the Soviet Union and these superior garments were known by soldiers as 'a present from the King of England'.

RIGHT:. Soviet soldiers work their way forwards through the rubble of Stalingrad. The wreckage of buildings hit by bombs and shell fire clogged the roads and blocked access for German tanks and armoured vehicles. Rubble helped conceal and protect bunkers and fortified cellars. The picture may have been posed, but it conveys a good sense of the restricted visibility in street fighting. Later in the war, the retreating Germans would deliberately destroy buildings to create rubble.

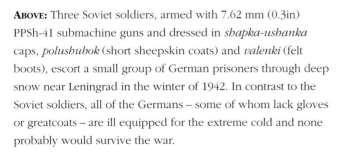

ABOVE: Three Soviet soldiers, armed with 7.62 mm (0.3in) PPSh-41 submachine guns and dressed in *shapka-ushanka* caps, *polushubok* (short sheepskin coats) and *valenki* (felt boots), escort a small group of German prisoners through deep snow near Leningrad in the winter of 1942. In contrast to the Soviet soldiers, all of the Germans – some of whom lack gloves or greatcoats – are ill equipped for the extreme cold and none probably would survive the war.

ABOVE:. A German soldier in December 1942 with an MG34 machine gun fitted onto a high-angle mount, the Dreifuss 34, and used in an AA role. The MG34 was 1219mm (48in) long and weighed 31.07kg (68.5lbs) on the sustained-fire mount. With a muzzle velocity of 755m (2477ft) a second, it had a maximum range of 2000m (2187yds) and a cyclic rate of 800–900 rounds per minute. It fired from a 75-round saddle drum magazine or 50-round non-disintegrating ammunition belts.

ABOVE: T-34/76D tanks of one of the sectors of Central Front in December 1942. The T-34/76D design incorporated lessons learned in combat with earlier marks of the T-34. It had a new hexagonal turret to eliminate the rear overhang and two hatches instead of one large one. It also had a single-horn periscope and a mushroom ventilator on the turret. Grab rails were welded to the turret to allow infantry to ride into action and spare fuel drums could be carried on the rear hull.

BELOW: Soviet soldiers firing a snow-camouflaged Field Howitzer Model 1910/30, a World War I veteran that was used in the early years of World War II. The crew from the South-Western Front is engaging targets in the winter of 1942. This howitzer had been upgraded in the 1930s to solid pneumatic tyred wheels, but many guns retained the metal-shod spoked wheels. The howitzer fired a 21.7kg (47.8lb) shell to a maximum range of 8940m (9777yds).

LEFT: In an improvised frontline workshop, men of Commander Boontman's repair unit lower into place the turret of a Light Wheel-Track Fast Tank BT-7 in the winter of 1942. The BT-7 had a top road speed of 74km/h (46mph) and was armed with a 45mm (1.77in) gun with up to 188 rounds and a 7.62mm (0.3in) machine gun with 2400 rounds. The BT tank earned the nickname *Betka* ('Beetle') or *Tri-Tankista* because of its three-man crew.

BELOW: With their helmets whitewashed as winter camouflage, German soldiers advance through a village supported by a Sturmgeschutz III Ausf E. SdKfz 142 assault gun. Armed with a short-barrelled 75mm (2.95in) gun, the Stug III had a crew of four. Although it had a very low silhouette, it had very limited traverse for the gun and was originally designed to give infantry close-range artillery support when attacking the enemy.

RIGHT: The minesweeper *Mina* of the Black Sea Fleet deploys on sweeping operations. The Romanian Navy had three mine-layers active in the Black Sea, which were reinforced by units from the Italian 10th Light Flotilla, and six U-boats that were shipped overland or down the Danube to the Romanian base at Constanta. This allied force was commanded by a (German) *Kriegsmarine* Admiral. Mine-laying operations would have restricted Soviet attempts to reinforce, resupply and evacuate casualties from the besieged ports of Odessa and Sevastopol.

ABOVE: A reserve formation of ski submachine gunners passes through a town on its way to the front in the late winter of 1942. Beneath their snow camouflage, the men would be wearing a padded *telogreika* or sheepskin jacket, padded trousers (*vatnie sharovari*), a *shapka-ushanka* fleece cap and sometimes *valenki* compressed-felt boots. A superior and much-prized version of these boots had a waterproof rubber sole. The clothing was basic, but very effective in extreme weather. The men are all carry PPSh-41 submachine guns. The short range of these weapons ensured that Soviet soldiers pressed home their attacks.

ABOVE: A tank crew in December 1942 stands by their T-34. The men wear the padded *telogreika* jackets and the fleece-lined padded tank crew helmet. Before the war, this helmet was constructed from black leather, but later it was replaced by black or grey canvas. The ear flaps are designed to allow an intercom headset to be worn. In summer, tank crews wore a one-piece coverall, the official colour of which was black, but it also appeared in grey and khaki.

ABOVE: Soviet Army signallers of the Central Front repair a telephone line in December 1942. Strong winds could snap telephone lines already weighed down with ice in Russian winters. Although the Soviet Army had radio communications, it was not as lavishly equipped as the Germans or the western Allies. Field telephones were used in the front line and the existing domestic network in the rear areas. In occupied territory, the telephone links were a relatively easy target for partisans to attack, which forced the Germans to use the radio, which was some-times unreliable due to the weather and also a less secure means of communication.

RIGHT:. Dressed in a white camouflage smock, with a hood deep enough to fit over his fur cap, a Soviet soldier armed with a PPSh-41 submachine gun waits in ambush in a birch forest on one of the sectors of the Central Front during the winter of 1942.

BELOW: Many 'combat' pictures taken by Soviet Army photographers were posed. This picture, taken during fighting in a town in Russia in December 1942, may in modern parlance have been 'stunted'. It does, however, encapsulate the confusion and violence of modern war. Steel-helmeted Soviet submachine gunners race hunched towards the smoke and dust that has enveloped a German position. The enemy may be stunned or dead, but the dust and smoke may also conceal men who will fight bitterly.

SNIPER WAR

Although snipers were used extensively by both sides throughout the war, Stalingrad was the perfect hunting ground for the men with telescopic sights. Hiding in the rubble of the city the snipers could pick off the unwary.

RIGHT: Cradling his 7.62mm (0.3in) Mosin Nagant M 1891/30 bolt-action rifle, a Soviet sniper with one of the frontline units of the 21st Army in Stalingrad in the winter of 1942–43. The rifle is fitted with the more powerful x 4 PE telescopic sight. Until 1930, the iron sights on the rifle were graduated in the archaic liner measurement of arshins, but the Soviet government redesigned the backsight in metres and the modified weapon became the 1891/30.

LEFT: Armed with a Tokarev SVT1940 automatic rifle fitted with a x 3.5 PV telescopic sight, a sniper on the Kalinin Front waits in ambush in 1942. He has chosen his position so that the scrub behind him breaks up his outline. His fur mitts have a single uninsulated trigger finger which allowed the weapon to be handled in extreme cold. Care had to be taken to ensure that this finger did not become frost-bitten. The Tokarev rifle weighed 3.95kg (8.7lbs) and had a 20-round magazine. Early models were unreliable, but the 1940 version was modified and eventually two million were manufactured.

RIGHT: A Soviet sniper at Stalingrad in the winter of 1942–43, with the modified 7.62mm (0.3in) Mosin Nagant M1891/30 rifle. In addition to having the x 4 PE sight offset on the left, to allow for the loading and ejection of rounds, the rifle has a longer bolt handle, turned down flush with the body. These are the only significant changes, however, to a rifle that in all other respects was the standard-issue weapon to infantry in the Soviet Army at the start World War II. The rifle owed its name to the designers, the Russian Colonel Serge I. Mosin and the Belgian Emil Nagant.

BELOW: Guards Junior Sergeant A. M. Yaremchoock of the Kalininsky Front operating as a sniper in 1942. He is armed with a Mosin Model 1891/30 rifle with a x 4 PE telescopic sight. The M1891/30 weighed 4kg (8.8lbs) empty, had a muzzle velocity of 811m/s (2661ft/s) and, although a modernisation of an old design, was robust and reliable. With a tradition of hunting in some extremely harsh terrain, soldiers conscripted from rural parts of the Soviet Union made excellent snipers.

ABOVE: A German PzKpfw II emerges from a forest on 9 December 1942. The tank, armed with a 20mm (0.79in) cannon, had been developed before the war. Delays in the production of the PzKpfw III and IV led to the II being used in campaigns in the West and later in Russia. It had a crew of three, weighed 9500kg (9.35tons) and its range was 200km (124.2 miles).

RIGHT: A Soviet artilleryman stands guard over 122mm (4.8in) howitzers in a depot in a wood on the Kalinin Front in 1942. Despite the snow, the crews have not covered the open muzzles. The casual approach to servicing and maintenance did not present a major problem in the Soviet Army because its weapons were robust and capable of withstanding abuse.

LEFT: Against the backdrop of a gutted factory which had turned into a fortress in Stalingrad, Soviet soldiers of the 62nd Army are addressed by their officers and political officers – *politicheskii rukovoditel, Politruk* or *Kommissar* (Commissar) – following the final capitulation of the German 6th Army in February 1943. The Soviet victory was a major propaganda boost for them, and marked a turning point in the war. A military or party official is on the right, distinguishable by his superior fur hat. One of the Commissars on the Stalingrad Front was Nikita Khruschev, a future leader of the postwar Soviet Union.

ABOVE: Wrapped in blankets and greatcoats, men of the defeated German 6th Army trudge away from Stalingrad in January 1943. The total human cost of Stalingrad to the Germans and their Axis allies was in the region of 1.5 million men. They also lost 3500 tanks, 12,000 guns and mortars, 75,000 vehicles and 3000 aircraft. With the smaller but significant Allied victory at El Alamein in North Africa, the war had begun its inexorable swing against Nazi Germany. In the summer of 1943, at Kursk, the Germans would make their final disastrous effort to wrest the strategic initiative from the Soviet Union.

RIGHT: A victorious Soviet soldier armed with a 7.62mm (0.3in) Mosin Nagant M 1891/30 bolt-action rifle, waves a red banner from a building overlooking Red Square in Stalingrad on 2 February 1943. On this date, the final German resistance in the northern pocket in the city ended, following the earlier surrender of Field Marshal Paulus on 31 January to the south. The remains of a German barricade can be seen below the soldier in the photograph, with captured vehicles parked behind it.

ABOVE: A park of abandoned German *Panzerjäger* 38(t) fuer 76.2mm (3in) Pak 36(r) Marder III self-propelled anti-tank guns captured at Stalingrad. The Marder III was a vehicle that combined captured Soviet 76.2mm (3in) FK 296 guns with the chassis of the Czech 38 (t) tank which had been obtained in large numbers by the Germans after the takeover, in 1939, of Czechoslovakia. Some 344 Marder IIIs were built and entered service in 1942. The vehicle had a crew of four, weighed 10,973kg (10.8 tons), had a maximum road speed of 42km/h (26mph) and its cross-country range was 160km (99 miles).

RIGHT: Field telephone lines snake through the trees on the east bank of the Volga. The postwar Communist version of the battle had Soviet soldiers willingly crossing the river by ferries and rafts to Stalingrad. The reality was that, looking across the wide river towards the blazing city, men realised that they were facing almost certain death. The NKVD security troops active on the east bank executed significant numbers of men who were reluctant to make the crossing, *pour encourager les autres.*

LEFT: Abandoned German trenches on the eastern edge of the Mamayev Kurgan, a 102m (335ft) high hill close to the eastern edges of Stalingrad that was once an ancient burial site, photographed after the Soviet victory. A pre-war beauty spot, it was bitterly contested by the 284th Division of the Soviet 62nd Army and the 295th Infantry Division of the 6th Army because it commanded an excellent view of the centre of the city. It was finally recaptured by the 284th Division in January 1943.

LEFT: A park of Marder III self-propelled anti-tank guns at Stalingrad. By the end of the fighting, the men of the German 6th Army were literally starving to death, ill equipped as they were for the severe cold. The promise of evacuation and resupply by air never truly materialised and, when the few airfields were captured, the Germans were doomed.

RIGHT: Boatmen of the 13th Guards Regiment on the partially frozen Volga unload ammunition. During the battle, most of this work was undertaken at great haste, under fire and at night. German flares, tracer fire and burning fuel on the water illuminated the crossing and many men drowned without reaching the far bank. Smaller boats such as these presented harder targets, even though they could carry less cargo. This scene may have been photographed after the Soviet victory.

LEFT: An abandoned German 150mm (5.9in) sFH18 howitzer battery on the Stalingrad perimeter in 1943. The guns have not been dug in and protected against counter-battery fire and so were probably moved to these positions after the onset of winter, when the frozen hard ground would make digging in impossible, as the 6th Army perimeter contracted under Soviet attacks. The horse teams that might have pulled the guns would have been slaughtered during the battle to provide meagre nourishment for the gun crews. This would have guaranteed that the guns would be lost when the time came to retreat further as the perimeter shrank around Stalingrad and German resistance weakened.

LEFT: A box-bodied truck parked on the east bank of the Volga in the winter of 1942–43. The Soviet GAZ-55 4 x 2 truck could be configured as an ambulance. However, unless this is an ambulance in position to receive casualties from ferries, it is more probable that this is a communications truck positioned close to the bank to ensure an uninterrupted radio link with the soldiers fighting on the far bank. Unless the Germans attempted to jam any transmissions, these links would have been excellent.

RIGHT: A cheerful Soviet T-34/76D tank crew wait on the bank of the Volga near Stalingrad in the early spring of 1943. The tank may have suffered a mechanical failure, as the engine louvres on the rear deck appear to be open. The tank is partially draped in a canvas sheet that may have been used as camouflage or to protect the crew against the cold. Pieces of timber and small rocks appear to have been placed under the tracks to assist the tank's movement across the shingle bank of the river.

ABOVE: A T-70 light tank of the Soviet 21st Army follows a T-34 in the fighting in the winter of 1942–43 in Stalingrad. The T-70 was armed with a 45mm (1.77in) gun and co-axial 7.62mm (0.3in) machine gun, but, with a maximum frontal armour of 40mm (1.57in), the crew would clearly be happier to have the more heavily armed and armoured T-34 at the front. The T-70 was built at the Gorki armaments plant, which normally specialised in trucks.

RIGHT: Lieutenant General V. I. Chuikov, commander of the 62nd Soviet Army and a member of the Military Council, talks to soldiers of the 39th Guards Rifle Division in front of his bunker in 1942–43.

CHAPTER FIVE

Crisis in the South

Prelude to Kursk

On 3 January 1943, the Germans began an urgent retreat from the Caucasus. Stalin had ordered his generals to drive for Rostov, in order to trap the German forces of Army Groups A and Don that had driven southeast to capture the oilfields in 1942. Operation Leap, proposed by Lieutenant General Nikolai Vatutin, commander of the South-West Front, would have locked a large number of Germans in Army Group A into the Donets basin.

LEFT: US-supplied Douglas A-20B Havoc light bombers of the Soviet Air Force flying in loose formation over the Ukraine in the late summer of 1942.

FAR LEFT: As smoke rises in the distance, a German soldier walks through the suburbs of the Black Sea town of Novorossiysk, which fell to 6th Army in September 1942.

DEATH ON THE DON

In fierce fighting on the Don River on 14 January, the men of the 2nd Hungarian Army suffered 70 per cent casualties. Despite these losses, Hitler demanded that Hungary provide more troops for the Eastern Front.

On 25 January, Stalin issued an Order of the Day to his troops, congratulating them and giving them the inspirational slogan: 'Onward to defeat the German occupationists.' He had promoted Zhukov to the rank of marshal a week earlier. Typically, Stalin, with no formal military training, decided that he too would become a marshal.

On 2 February, Zhukov and the Chief of the Soviet Staff, Vasilevsky, launched the Voronezh Front into a two-pronged attack code-named Operation Star. It was intended to go southwest past Kharkov towards the Dneipr and northwest via Kursk towards Smolensk. That month, the versatile Yak-9 fighter entered service with the Red Air Force.

On 16 February, Kharkov fell to the advancing Soviet forces of General Filip Golikov's Voronezh Front and Vatutin's South-West Front. The city had been abandoned by three Waffen-SS Panzer divisions tasked with its defence. They had broken out to the south and fought over 186km (116 miles) to link up with General Herman Hoth's 4th Panzer Army. It made sound military sense – Kharkov had been encircled and the garrison had also to contend with an uprising by the population. Hitler, however, demanded that the city should be recaptured.

So, four days later, the *Waffen-SS* went back onto the offensive. Disobeying an order from Hoth to bypass the city, they plunged back into it on 11 March and, four days later, Kharkov was again in German hands.

KHARKOV COUNTERATTACK

The operation at Kharkov was part of a counterattack of the the two Soviet fronts' southern flanks by Army Group South, commanded by Field Marshal Manstein. The attack, again spearheaded by the *Waffen-SS*, inflicted heavy losses and forced the Soviet troops back behind the River Donets. To the south, Operation Leap had overextended itself and ended when, on 18 February, the 1st Panzer Army demolished Vatutin's mobile group.

Part of the reason for Manstein's triumph at Kharkov may have been his close tactical control of the fast-moving battle; there were no long, encoded Enigma signals back to Hitler's HQ at Rastenburg in East Prussia, signals that were the undoing of many German plans, since they were intercepted and decoded by Station X at Bletchley Park.

LEFT: The battleship *Pariskaya Kommuna*, formerly the *Sevastopol* of the Black Sea Fleet, firing its 300mm (11.8in) main armament at German and Romanian positions in the Crimea. The *Pariskaya Kommuna* sailed from the Baltic in 1930 and it was reported before the war that she was unfit to make the return journey. With her sister, the *Marat*, she was completed in 1914 and later refitted; however, she was said to be a dreadful ship to live in, with practically no ventilation.

BELOW: Soviet soldiers examine a knocked-out German PzKpfw IV Ausf E tank that appears to have crashed off a bridge in the winter of 1942. Innovative Panzer leader General Heinz Guderian was the driving force behind the PzKpfw IV's development, which he saw as a heavy support vehicle. It became the mainstay of operations in the Soviet Union. Its chassis would be used for self-propelled, flak and assault guns.

LEFT: Resembling a fort built in the Wild West, a German guard post beside a railway in Russia in the winter of 1942–43. The woods have been cleared back from the track to give soldiers in the observation tower a clear view down the line. Similar positions, with a garrison of about 20 men, would have been constructed at regular intervals along the track. Although these guard posts could provide some security in daylight, the lines would have been vulnerable to attack by night from the large numbers of partisans beginning to operate behind the German lines.

ABOVE: A turretless PzKpfw IV tank destroyed on the outskirts of Zhitomir in the Ukraine in the winter of 1943. The extensive damage suggests that it first caught fire and then exploded as the 87 rounds of 75mm (2.96in) and machine-gun ammunition, six hand grenades and 24 signal flares stowed onboard detonated.

BELOW: Dressed in winter camouflage, Soviet soldiers of the Kalinin Front crawl towards a German position in the winter of 1942-43. Soviet soldiers armed with rifles or submachine guns developed a technique of crawling dragging the weapon beside them with the sling hooked in the crook of the finger and thumb.

LEFT: Soviet soldiers of the Kalinin Front take aim with their PPSh-41 submachine guns holding the 3.56 kg weapon so that the 71 round drum magazine clear of the ground. The men do not appear to be wearing gloves – this would make weapon handling easier, but the metal of the magazine or barrel would be dangerously cold. In Arctic conditions bare hands could freeze to metal in moments. The soldiers wisely therefore hold the wooden stock and butt of the weapon.

RIGHT: Soviet soldiers of the 3rd Shock Army fighting through the streets of Velikie Luki on the River Lovat in January 1943. Defended by the 83rd Infantry Division and 277th Grenadier Regiment, it was held against repeated assaults from November 1942 to January 1943. There were two attempts to relieve the besieged German garrison, but it was finally overwhelmed. Only one man, Lieutenant Behnemann of the 183rd Artillery Regiment, escaped.

BELOW: Soviet T-34/76D tanks on the move in a road convoy. Good roads could increase the range and speed of tanks. With its 500 hp V-2-34 12 cylinder diesel, the T-34 had a top cross-country speed of 40km/h (24.9mph); on roads, this went up to 54 km/h (33.5mph). Range increased from 300km (186 miles) to 400km (248 miles) on roads.

ABOVE: Women and children queue for water on the edge of the frozen River Neva, during the siege of Leningrad in the winter of 1942–43. Almost the entire population of the city was mobilised by Lieutenant General A. A. Zhadanov, the Secretary of the Soviet Central Committee. This included 600,000 juveniles and children, who, with adults, were put to work building some of the 880km (547 miles) of anti-tank ditches and 5000 earth bunkers that were part of the defences.

RIGHT: Nuriy Shakirov, a sniper with the 207th Rifle Regiment of the Soviet 21st Army in the South-Western Front, takes aim through the x 4 PE telescopic sight on his 7.62 mm (0.3in) Mosin Nagant M1891/30 rifle. The sights on the rifle were offset, mounted on the left of the receiver, to allow the empty cases to be ejected when the bolt was worked. Soviet snipers usually worked in pairs at a low tactical level, and were assigned directly to companies and platoons in the front line.

A BRIEF RESPITE

After the strangulation and destruction of the 6th Army at Stalingrad and the counterattacks in the winter of 1942–43, the onset of the spring thaw and consequent mud brought a halt to operations.

On 18 February 1943, following the surrender of the 6th Army at Stalingrad, Goebbels addressed a picked audience at the *Sportpalastrede*, the Sports Palace in Berlin. Under a huge banner that read *Totaler Krieg für Zester Krieg* (Total War for Shortest War), he gave a powerful speech, carrying his audience with him as they pledged themselves for combat and sacrifice.

Goebbels hurled 10 questions at the fanaticised crowd, to which they thundered back the answer 'Ja!' (Yes!) The last question the Propaganda Minister posed was 'Do you want total war?' When the affirmation was roared back, Goebbels replied with the words of the great call to war in 1812, 'Let Our War-Cry Be: Now the People Rise Up and the Storm Break Loose!'

On 1 March, Army Group Centre began an operation code-named Buffalo. This was the phased withdrawal from the extended Rzhev salient opposite Moscow. Even Hitler now agreed that it was no longer a credible threat to the Soviet capital. By 23 March the Germans halted on a line from Velizh to Kirov. They had cut their frontage by nearly 400km (249 miles) and freed enough troops to keep Rokossovsky in check by creating a reserve able to plug and gaps that might appear in the German line.

KATYN UNCOVERED

On 26 May 1943 German forces discovered mass graves at a forest at Katyn near Smolensk. They contained the bodies of 4500 Polish officers captured by the Russians in 1939 during the division of Poland between Germany and Russia. They had been bound and shot in the back of the head by the

ABOVE: Warmly dressed in his sheepskin coat and *shapka-ushanka* cap, the young officer A. V. Chapaev, son of the commander of the 25th Rifle Division, V. I. Chapaev, with Lieutenant Colonel Kupin in the streets of Kharkov in February 1943.

ABOVE: A smashed German locomotive lies on its side after it triggered a buried charge laid beneath the tracks by partisans in an area in the occupied Ukraine. Attacks like this not only destroyed engines and rolling stock and disrupted the flow of reinforcements and supplies, but also made the rear areas a war zone in which German troops were not safe. To counter these operations, the Germans patrolled the tracks and had static guard posts at key points. Naturally this tied up large numbers of troops who could have been better occupied (from the German point of view) on the front line.

NKVD before being unceremoniously buried. For the Nazis this was a propaganda coup, and they tried hard to exploit it to create division among the Soviets and the Western Allies. However, the work of a neutral commission established to determine the truth behind the massacres was interrupted when German forces were forced to withdraw from the position by the Soviet advance in September 1943.

HITLER OPTIMISTIC

Despite the huge losses sustained by the Wehrmacht following the surrender at Stalingrad, Hitler remained optimistic. He had just over three million soldiers in Russia – slightly more in fact than had launched the invasion in June 1941 – and new weapons and equipment were beginning to reach them in the front line. Operation Buffalo had yielded an extra army, the 9th Army, which, under the vigorous command of the monocled General Walther Model, had for 14 months held the toughest part of the Eastern Front, the line around Rzhev.

The 4th Panzer Army had been reinforced with three new *Waffen-SS* panzer divisions fully equipped with the superior Panther and Tiger tanks. The Tiger was armed with a formidable 88mm (3.45in) gun, while the Panther, with a crew of five, weighed 45.5 tonnes and had a maximum speed of 46km/h (29mph). The tank's sloped armour ranged from 110mm (4.3in) to 30mm (1.1in) in thickness, and it was armed with a 75mm (2.95in) gun and two 7.92mm (0.31in) machine guns.

With the onset of summer, Hitler was confident that a rearmed and rested Germany would win back the initiative in Russia. What is more, it seemed the Wehrmacht could create a Russian Stalingrad – at Kursk.

LEFT: Soviet gunners load an M1942 ZIS-3 76mm (3in) gun covering down a road. The crew for such a gun was normally six to seven men, so this gun has minimum manning, which would slow the rate of fire. The gun was mounted on a 57mm (2.25in) carriage and could fire a range of high-explosive and armour-piercing ammunition; the maximum range with high explosive was 13,290m (14,534yds). The high-explosive anti-tank (HEAT) round weighed 4kg (8.8lbs), had a muzzle velocity of 325m/s (1066ft/s) and could penetrate 120mm (4.72in) of armour.

BELOW: Soviet soldiers in the basic summer order march through a village in central Russia. They wear *pilotka* caps and have BN gas-mask haversacks slung on their left hips and M1938 packs. Most carry M1891/30 Mosin Nagant rifles, but one man has a Pulemet Degtyareva Pekhotnii (DP) light machine gun. They wear ankle boots and their legs are wrapped in puttees made from cloth from worn-out uniforms. Their greatcoats, rolled and slung across their shoulders, hold items of spare clothing.

RIGHT: Using the hull of a knocked-out German PzKpfw IV tank for overhead cover, a group of Soviet officers from the South-Western Front have established a forward observation post from which to study German positions in the spring of 1943. The Germans copied the Soviet technique of digging in under knocked-out armoured vehicles in the fighting in Normandy in 1944 after the D-Day landings. It offered excellent protection against artillery and mortar fire, and was safe as long as the tank did not settle in soft ground.

ABOVE: *Tyazholy Tank KV* – Heavy Tank 'Klimenti Voroshilov' or KV-1 tanks – of the 6th Soviet Tank Regiment on the march with their regimental banner. The KV-1 had a 76.2mm (3.0in) M1940 gun and three 7.62mm (0.3in) machine guns. It was heavily armoured, but even this was upgraded with extra plates bolted to the hull and turret. Despite this increase in weight, the tank was still powered by a V-2K-s 12-cyl water-cooled diesel developing 600hp. Production of the KV-1 ceased in 1943.

CHAPTER SIX

Kursk

The Clash of Armour

The fighting in Russia normally slowed with the spring thaw, which produced immobility as the roads turned to soft mud. After Kharkov, the front line stabilised into a huge Soviet salient 190km (118 miles) wide and 120km (75 miles) deep which had the railway city of Kursk at its centre. The planned German summer offensive of 1943 aimed to pinch out this bulge with attacks from the north by Army Group Centre, under Kluge, and the south by Army Group South, under Manstein. The attacks would be codenamed *Unternehmen Zitadelle* (Operation Citadel).

LEFT: Soviet gunners with their dug-in 76.2mm (3.0in) Field Gun Model 02/30 with its longer L/40 barrel, which was installed when the Model 1902 Putilov guns were modernised in 1930.

FAR LEFT: Armourer Sergeant Majors Starshina N. Titiov and A. Reva of the Russian Air Force prepare to load captured German SC-250 bombs onto a Petlyakov Pe-2.

LUCY AND ULTRA

Possibly the greatest triumph of ULTRA was the interception of the plans for Citadel, which were passed to the Soviet Union through the 'Lucy' spy ring in Switzerland. The spy ring was operated by Sandor Rado, who was assisted by Rudolf Rössler, a Protestant Bavarian journalist. Intelligence may also have come from the head of the Abwehr, Admiral Canaris, but the detailed, high-grade material which ULTRA supplied was to give the Red Army a massive advantage when the Germans finally attacked the salient in July. The Lucy ring was a convenient way of filtering this information to the Soviet Union, which was not privy to the top-secret code-breaking operation in Britain. Until details of the ULTRA operation became public in the 1970s, the Lucy ring was assumed to have had contacts deep inside the OKW.

The German plan was not as ambitious as the offensives of 1941 and 1942. Nevertheless, Hitler thought it would give Germany psychological leverage after Stalingrad and 'light a bonfire' that would impress the world and possibly intimidate the Soviet High Command.

The Germans gathered 900,000 men and 2700 tanks and armoured vehicles, including Tiger and Panther tanks. Kursk would be the operational debut of the Panther. Some 2000 aircraft were deployed on the shoulders of the salient.

WAFFEN-SS — A BRUTAL ELITE

The cream of the *Waffen-SS* (Armed SS) was to fight at Kursk. The *Waffen-SS* was the military arm and largest branch of the SS - eventually numbering 39 divisions – through the ranks of which passed nearly one million men of 15 nationalities. It took part in 12 major battles and was noted for its tough fighting qualities and aggressive leadership. Its premier formation, the *Leibstandarte Adolf Hitler* (Adolf Hitler's bodyguard), provided guards of honour for visiting VIPs before the war. The *Waffen-SS* saw little action in Poland, but fought in France, the Balkans and Russia.

The attack at Kursk was first scheduled to begin on 4 May, but was cancelled and reinstated for 5 July 1943. Hitler confessed that he was worried that it would not achieve the same level of surprise as offensives in previous years. He was right to be concerned. To counter the attack, the Soviet High Command, Stavka, deployed 20,000 guns, 3300 tanks, 2560 aircraft and one and a third million troops. Anti-tank guns, mines and infantry bunkers were grouped in armour killing grounds called *Pakfronts*. The minefields were designed to channel the German tanks towards the anti-tank guns and, if they broke through one layer of defences, there was another behind it. The density of mines was massive, at 2500 anti-personnel mines and 2200 anti-tank mines per 1.6km (1 mile) of front. In all, there were six belts of three to five trench lines about 40km (25 miles) deep. Marshal Zhukov planned to break the impetus of the German attack and then launch Operations Kutuzov and Rumyantsev, massive counterattacks to the north and south using men and tanks held in reserve.

ARTILLERY STRIKE

So detailed was the Soviet knowledge of the German plan that they launched an artillery bombardment just before the German assault was due to go in. German radar detected the Red Air Force units en route to attack and the Luftwaffe intercepted them, and so achieved local air superiority.

On the ground, the German 9th Army under Field Marshal von Kluge only achieved minor successes against a determined Soviet defence and suffered 25,000 casualties. To the south, Field Marshal von Manstein's 4th Panzer Army made better headway, pushing forwards 40km (25 miles). On 12 July, the 2nd SS Panzer Corps reached Prokhorovka and encountered the 5th Guards Tank Army, part of the Stavka reserve. In the ensuing maelstrom of dust, smoke and flames, about 1200 tanks fought the largest tank battle of the war and possibly the largest in history.

The Allied landings in Sicily on 10 July prompted Hitler to order a halt to Operation Citadel. He insisted that the 2nd SS Panzer Corps, which he rated as the equivalent of 20 Italian divisions, should be withdrawn and sent south to Italy to halt the Allied landings.

Two days later, Operation Kutuzov (the Soviet counterattack in the north by the West Front and Bryansk Front) was launched and the exhausted German 9th and 2nd Panzer Armies fell back. To the south, Operation Rumyantsev (the attack by the Voronezh Front and Steppe Front) was launched on 3 August. The 4th Panzer Army and Operational Group *Kempf* fought a hard action as they withdrew, counterattacking and delaying the Soviet advance, but not halting it. By the end of the fighting, each side had lost about 1500 tanks; however, unlike the German tanks, many of the Soviet ones could be recovered and repaired.

ABOVE: Lightly equipped Soviet soldiers of the 13th Guards Division scramble from a trench during the fighting at Kharkov in 1943. Two are armed with the PPSh-41 submachine gun, but one man, probably an NCO, has the superb 7.62mm (0.3in) Samozariadnyia Vintovka Tokareva o1940g or SVT40 automatic rifle. When German soldiers captured SVT40s, they were quick to put them back into use against their former owners, re-designating them A1Gew259(r). The drawback with the SVT40 was that it had a heavy recoil. The rifle had a 10-round box magazine and weighed 3.89kg (8.58lbs).

LEFT: A Soviet Air Force major, probably the pilot, begins to pull on his parachute as the crew of a US-supplied North American B25J Mitchell bomber prepares for a mission in the Krasnodar region on 29 May 1943. The Soviets received 862 B25B/D/G and J Mitchells during the course of the war. The US policy on supplying equipment to the Soviet Union was to send only aircraft, weapons or vehicles that they knew that the Germans had already encountered in battle and captured in the West

RIGHT: Major D. Korolenko of the Steppe Front, a recipient of the Defence of Stalingrad Medal, mans a field telephone with his female signaller in the Kharkov region in 1943. The map spread in front of Korolenko suggests that they are an artillery forward observation post and he is correcting fire for a battery by sending them the grid references on which they are to fire. If the rounds fell short or long of the target, he could then advise them on the corrections needed to hit the target. An observation post would necessarily be within sight of the target to give accurate ranging information; the two soldiers shown here, however, look rather more relaxed than the occupants of a frontline trench.

LEFT: Dust and smoke boil up as a Soviet 152mm (6in) M1937 (ML-20) gun howitzer comes into action near Kharkov in 1943. To the left, one of the crew of 10 carries a shell case on his shoulder and, in the foreground, an empty case has been thrown clear of the gun pit. An experienced crew could keep up a rate of four rounds per minute. The M1937 weighed 7128kg (15,715lbs) in the firing position and, firing the 43.6kg (96.1lb) high-explosive round, it had a maximum range of 17,300m (18,920yds).

RIGHT: Naval Infantry or *Morskaia Pekhota* of the Black Sea Fleet commanded by G. Slennev fighting through the northeastern suburbs of Novorossiysk in June 1943. A 7.62mm (0.3in) Pulemet Maksima Obrazets 1910 Maxim machine gun in the ruins appears to be giving rather hazardous covering fire – the shallower the angle, the greater the risk that the fire will hit friendly forces.

LEFT: Soviet troops on the march in the summer of 1943. The man in the centre is armed with the Pulemet Degtyareva Pekhotnii (DP) light machine gun. The gun, designed in the 1920s by Vasily Alexeyevich Degtyarev, was a simple gas-operated weapon with only six moving parts. It fired from a 47-round drum magazine at 520 to 580 rounds a minute and weighed 11.9kg (26.2lbs). It remained in service with guerrilla forces in Asia and Africa into the 1970s.

RIGHT: A column of T-34/76D tanks grinds through a Ukrainian village in the summer of 1943. The lead vehicle appears to have some rudimentary camouflage attached to the hull. On the open steppe, there were often few opportunities to site or camouflage a vehicle so that it could not be observed from the air. Villages and farms, or the steep *balka* (gullies), were the only places where there was some protective cover from both view and fire.

LEFT: Abandoned after their combat debut at Kursk in July 1943, German PzKpfw V Ausf D Panther tanks knocked out by the 1st Ukrainian Front. The Panthers had been rushed into action and many suffered mechanical break-downs and problems with their tracks. The PzKpfw V Ausf D had a crew of five and was armed with a 75mm (2.95in) KwK42 (L/70) gun with 79 rounds and one coaxial 7.92mm (0.31in) MG34 machine gun. Later marks had a hull machine gun and an AA mount by the commander's hatch.

RIGHT: A column of Soviet T-34/85 ob.1943 tanks of the 20th Guards Tanks commanded by S. F. Shutov moves through the wheat lands of the western Ukraine in the summer of 1943 after the failure of the German Kursk offensive. The T-34/85 was described by the Germans at the time as 'the best tank in the world'. It had a crew of five and was armed one 85mm (3.35in) ZIS S-53 gun with 55 rounds and two 7.62mm (0.3in) machine guns, one hull-mounted and one coaxial with 2394 rounds. The main armament was capable of knocking out the majority of German armour it might encounter. The T-34/85 could move at 35km/h 21.7mph) across country and 50km/h (31mph) on roads, with a range of 300km (186 miles).

RIGHT: T-34/76 tanks of the 6th Guards Army of the Voronezh Front with 'tank descent' troops riding on the hull, at Kursk in July 1943. Interestingly, the tank is the older 1941 model with its large single-turret hatch. The infantry on board do not have the benefit of the hand rails which were welded to later marks of the T-34. The dismantled tractor factories that were moved to the Urals in 1941 became the huge 'Tankograd' complex, the main manufacturing plant for tanks for the Soviet Army in the war.

LEFT: Wearing his padded tank crew helmet, or *tankobyi shlem*, Hero of the Soviet Union, Lieutenant I. I. Burschick of the 1st Czech Corps with the Soviet Army stands in front of a T-34 following the battle of Kursk. During the fighting, his crew was reported to have destroyed six PzKpfw VI Tigers and four *Panzerjäger* Tiger (P) Elephant self-propelled anti-tank guns. The Elephant was armed with the powerful 88mm (3.46in) Pak 43/2/L/71 gun, but had no hull machine gun and hence was incredibly vulnerable to Soviet infantry anti-tank crews.

LEFT: Soviet Air Force ground crew examine battle damage to the port wing of an Ilyushin DB-3F bomber of the Western Front parked in its revetment bay in 1943. Lack of equipment or the rather casual style of the Soviet armed forces has meant that the men have not erected a work platform to gain access to the wing, but rather have simply climbed onto it. Robust as combat aircraft may be, if the bomber was damaged, the weight of almost three men at the extremity of the wing would certainly not assist its structural integrity. The aircraft on the field have been given the protection of earth revetments, but by this stage of the war the Soviet air arm was dominant in the skies over the Soviet Union.

LEFT: A T-34/76D gives a Soviet infantry squad a ride towards the front. The soldiers are sitting high on the turret in and out of the two hatches, the infantry wear their cotton drill *pilotka* side hats and have their rifles slung. The driver of the tank has his access hatch wide open for improved visibility and fresh air. These are men pictured in the summer of 1943, at their ease some distance from the front line and the threat of any enemy action.

LEFT: Soviet BT-7 light tanks captured by the Germans early in the war are clearly marked with national insignia on turret and hatches to avoid 'friendly fire'. These damaged vehicles abandoned on a section of the Kalinin Front in 1943 appear to have been positioned to cover a bridge, perhaps part of a screen for a German withdrawal. The 45mm (1.77in) gun might have been effective against infantry in the open, but it was no match for the thick armour of the T-34s.

ABOVE: A 'Herbert' pontoon bridge more than one kilometre (three-fifths of a mile) long, built by German engineers near Kharkov in the Ukraine in August 1943. The 'Herbert' bridge was constructed from steel-lattice pyramid panels made of angle iron which bolted together and were supported either by pontoons or trestles. The decking was made from 155mm (0.6in) timber planking and the road was 4m (4.37yds) wide. The Germans classified the bridge as capable of taking a load of 18 tonnes over 30m (33yds).

BELOW: Headed by an officer in the high-crowned Don Cossack black fleece cap or *papkha*, steel-helmeted Soviet cavalry trot past a river in the North Caucasus in August 1943. The Cossack cavalry could harry enemy infantry in retreat.

CHAPTER SEVEN

The Partisan War

War in the Shadows

Russian partisan warfare and resistance began by accident, as Soviet soldiers cut off by the German attacks found themselves effectively behind enemy lines. The first steps towards organised resistance were taken by the Central Committee of the Belorussian Communist Party, headed by P. K. Ponomarenko. Since 50 per cent of partisans were initially party members, NKVD officers or members of the *Komsomol* (Young Communists), they were at a marked disadvantage in rural areas where peasants feared and distrusted the party. In the Ukraine, the partisans were completely wiped out because of the hostility of the local population and they found it difficult to operate in the Crimea and the steppes.

Ideally, partisans required a passive or friendly local population who would provide intelligence and food. Night-time parachute drops would bring supplies of weapons and ammunition, and further supplies would be captured in ambushes and by theft. Dense woods, swamps or mountains were essential to provide safe areas in which the partisans could hide, train or nurse the wounded.

Initially, successful operations were undertaken around the cities of Yelnia and Dorogobuzh east of Smolensk, mostly conducted by Red Army stragglers. The second phase of partisan resistance lasted until the end of 1942, when the surviving elements of the Political Administration of the Red Army (PURKKA) brought the Red Army groups under central control. NKVD officers and Young Communist members were parachuted into occupied areas to assist PURKKA. Stalin, meanwhile, demanded that the partisans not become a force that was not controlled by Moscow.

LEFT: A small group of partisans emerges from the cover of a young fir forest in late winter. Huge forests and swamps such as the Pripet Marshes provided cover.

FAR LEFT: A young partisan Pulemet Degtyareva Pekhotnii (DP) light machine gunner. The rather flimsy construction of the 47-round gun magazine can be seen. The DP was a simple gas-operated weapon, ideal for use by the relatively unsophisticated partisans.

BATTLE OF THE RAILWAYS

In the third phase of resistance, however, the partisans began to take the war to their occupiers, concentrating on road and rail links. Railways were blown up and roads mined; if the repair teams were inadequately protected, they could, in turn, be ambushed. After the victory at Stalingrad, partisans began to penetrate the Briansk region and were strong around the fringes of the Pripet marshes. Their attacks hampered German operations during the battle of Kursk. Other groups infiltrated the woods and swamps towards the River Dniepr and the wooded areas of the northern Ukraine. Before and during the Red Army's Belorussian campaign in 1944, the partisans were successful in their attacks on road and rail links.

German tactics to counter the partisans included passive measures such as defending railway goods yards and depots, and patrolling roads. They also conducted anti-partisan drives and here it was the population that often suffered. Areas that were believed to be partisan hide-outs were cordoned off and searched. Both the partisans and the Germans executed civilians for collaborating and attempted to terrorise them into passivity or active assistance. The destruction of villages and execution of their populations was an all too common tactic of revenge.

In 1943, the *Waffen-SS* officer who had rescued Mussolini, Otto Skorzeny, formed battalion-sized anti-partisan and special operations groups known as *Jagdverbände* (JV, or Hunting Units). These units were based in various places in Europe and named after the operational area, thus there were Eastern, Southeastern and Western *Jagdverbände*.

Figures vary widely as to the numbers of partisans that fought in the western Soviet Union. Not all the armed bands behind the German lines were partisans. Gangs of escaped prisoners of war and deserters became bandits evading the NKVD, as well as German forces. The Germans estimated that there were between 400,000 and 500,000 partisans. Other sources say 700,000, while the Soviet histories put it as high as one million. On a monthly basis, there were probably 250,000 partisans in action and, during the war, the partisans killed about 35,000 Axis soldiers.

Although the effectiveness of the partisans may have been exaggerated for propaganda purposes, their operations had a profound psychological effect on the German and Axis soldiers in the Soviet Union.

ABOVE: Partisans with horse-drawn wagons and cattle move through a village in western Russia. The partisans' mobility was confined to horses and marching, so weapons were largely rifles and submachine guns, with some mortars and machine guns.

ABOVE: While one man armed with a PPSh-41 submachine gun keeps watch, a Soviet partisan explosives specialist prepares a timber bridge for demolition. In World War II, the Soviet armed forces would not have access to plastic explosives and therefore the specialist would have to wire a slab of TNT to the piers supporting the bridge. Although the rivers appears shallow and therefore not a major obstacle, the destruction of the bridge would nonetheless slow down German movement.

RIGHT: Partisans wade across a shallow stream in the summer on 1942. The close-cropped hair and age of the man in the foreground suggests that he is a Soviet soldier who has escaped from a battle of encirclement and joined the partisans. His weapons handling skills and experience would be invaluable to the group. Initially, many of the partisan groups consisted largely of soldiers who had evaded capture or had managed to escape from captivity. Behind the former soldier, a female fighter plods forwards with a medal prominently displayed on her blouse. It was common for women to fight in the Partisans.

ABOVE: In a secure area behind German lines, partisans cross a frozen lake. If there had been an enemy air threat, they would have skirted the lake – now, in their dark-coloured clothes, they stand out clearly against the snow and later their tracks will remain, although by walking in a narrow column it will be difficult for anyone tracking them to estimate their numbers. Each man has a simple pack made from a grain sack which is secured at the neck by a cord which is linked to the corners. Although winter may have been harsh, the long hours of darkness provided excellent cover for groups to attack or evade capture.

LEFT: A partisan group armed with the Pulemet Degtyareva Tankovii (DT) light machine gun, in the Kursk area of the Ukraine, waits in ambush in the late winter of 1942. The DT was originally designed for use as anti-aircraft (AA) armament on tanks and weighed 12.69 kg (27.98lbs). It had an adjustable metal butt, a 60-round drum magazine and fired at 600 rounds a minute. In the extreme Russian winters and summers, magazine-fed automatic weapons had the advantage over belt-fed, as they were less likely to foul.

BELOW: With his PPSh-41 submachine gun stuck butt first into the snow to prevent it fouling and the metal becoming intensely cold, Commander Bocharov, assisted by E. V. Frantzusov, prepares a line for demolition in the Maloyaroslavskiy district near Moscow in 1942. The PPSh-41was known by many soldiers by its initials as the 'Paypay Shay'. Two partisans stand as guards and lookouts, while the demolition man uses a bayonet to dig out the snow and ballast under the track.

ABOVE: A group of partisans receives a briefing from their commander. The picture looks rather contrived, with one of the kneeling officers wearing his medals during this conference in a woodland base. One entirely authentic feature is the man at the back on the left, who is armed with a captured German 9mm (0.35in) MP38/40 submachine gun, loosely known as the Schmeisser. The partisans used captured weapons, ammunition and medical stores, in addition to those delivered by air.

RIGHT: Partisans leading ponies cross a bridge in the spring of 1942. Ponies gave the partisans the advantage of being able to move quickly, and could cross terrain that German vehicles could not. However ponies require both food and water, and supplies either have to be carried or found when camping for the night, a fact which could counterbalance the advantage of their speed of movement. Both sides made use of animals during the war, and German anti-partisan patrols could often be mounted on horseback for ease of movement.

LEFT: Sunlight glints off the clear plastic overlay on a partisan officer's map case, as he confers with colleagues on the fringes of a wood. Some groups were led by forceful and imaginative leaders, but the German policy of forced deportation of labour meant that other groups contained less motivated men, those simply on the run evading conscription as *Ost Arbeiters* (Eastern Workers). After the Soviet liberation of the Ukraine, there were even partisan groups who saw Stalin as a worse ogre than Hitler and who fought for the Germans, ambushing small convoys and mining roads.

BELOW: In a forest base, a partisan radio operator taps out a Morse message while an assistant wearing a 'Kirov' peaked cap logs the incoming traffic. The radio's wire antenna can be seen running from the set up into the trees. Experienced operators would climb high into trees and align the antenna towards a receiving station to achieve a clear signal. They would also become very efficient Morse operators, capable of sending and receiving messages at great speed.

LEFT: In the autumn chill, a small group of partisans keeps warm by a fire. In areas of deep woodland where groups were secure, they were able to build semi-permanent log camps. In the winter, some partisans even constructed bathhouses for cleaning bodies and disinfecting clothes. Here, a former zoology teacher in one group is showing his comrades how, in the summer, wood ants would eat lice on clothing which had been placed on ant hills, cleaning a garment in about five minutes.

RIGHT: Wooden buildings burn as a partisan group fights through a German held collective farm. The picture looks suspiciously posed, as, while the man on the right wearing the Soviet Army *pilotka* cap has taken cover and appears to be shooting at the burning building, he is dangerously close to his comrades, who are in a very exposed position as they crouch on the open ground. The photograph seems to have been taken by a man who would be have been standing in a very exposed position himself if a real fire fight was in progress. The partisans, once they had been brought under Moscow's control, proved to be a useful propaganda tool for the Soviets. However, while some groups were feared and respected by the Germans, others were much less effective.

LEFT: Ducking for cover amongst the saltwater marshes of the Kuban, Soviet partisans conduct a fighting withdrawal after shooting up a German position in April 1943. If this is an authentic picture, the German mortar crew appears to have got the range of their fleeting enemies and the cameraman nerves of steel. However, a comparatively modest explosive charge covered with a sack of soot will, when detonated, produce a geyser of black dirt that looks quite convincing as mortar fire.

LEFT: Protected by the shield, a partisan of the Stchors Zhitomir group puts down supporting fire with his Maxim 1910 water-cooled machine gun in the summer of 1943. On its wheeled Sokolov mount with the shield, this was a far from mobile weapon, weighing 74kg (163lbs); however, in the defensive phases of the war in Russia, this was less of a problem. Later, the shield was discarded to save weight. The gun was very accurate, partly because of the mount and also because of its slow rate of fire of only 550 rounds a minute.

BELOW: In a scene that looks as if it was taken from a Hollywood Western, horsemen and wagons of A. N. Saburov's Soviet partisan group ford a river in the Zhitomir area in the spring of 1943. The size of the formation and its relaxed manner show either a reckless disregard for security or that the partisan group had expanded and now dominates the area. The wagons would be used for support weapons, ammunition and medical equipment; each mounted partisan would be self-sufficient.

RIGHT: Keeping their boots dry, Soviet partisan infantry of the Zhitomir group commanded by A. N. Saburov wade a river in the spring of 1943. Although dressed in largely civilian clothes, the man on the left of the photograph proudly wears a military medal. Wet leather can take a very long time to dry and the water could damage the boots. There would be limited opportunities for boot repairs in a partisan group that relied on mobility and the remote locations of its bases to ensure safety and security from enemy attack. Oil for the boots would also be in short supply – one of the reasons the PPSh-41 was so effective as a partisan weapon was its chromed barrel, which needed far less maintenance and care than an uncoated one.

LEFT: Soviet partisans of the Zhitomir group commanded by A. N. Saburov ford a river in 1943. By this time, partisan groups were better organised and properly supported by Stavka headquarters staff in Moscow. Among the weapons in this group are PPSh-41 submachine guns, which may have been parachuted to the group. With explosives, mines and new weapons at their disposal, partisans would be able to play a significant part of the battle of Kursk in the summer of 1943.

RIGHT: The speed and urgency of an attack by the *Za Pobedu* ('To Victory') partisan group against a railway during the 'Railway War' launched by Stavka, the Soviet High Command, on 14 July 1943 is caught in this photograph. As M. A. Tarasov in the foreground covers down the track, the demolitions specialist A. Y. Budishevskiy gets quickly to work by this level crossing. The Germans used dogs to detect explosives, so, to throw them off the scent, the partisans scattered tiny pieces of explosives along railway tracks.

LEFT: A German-held building burns as, with sabres drawn, mounted partisans of the Stchors Zhitomir group launch an attack on Ignatopol railway station in the Ukraine in the spring of 1943. These horsemen might well be cavalry soldiers, who with the mobility of their mounts were able to evade capture by Germans in 1941 or 1942 and have brought their skills and experience to enhance the power and flexibility of the partisan group.

BELOW: A Soviet nurse bandages a partisan with a chest wound. The careful way the Red Cross bag has been positioned and the nurse's head scarf look rather contrived; however, this should not detract from the courageous work these women undertook in the front line, sometimes under fire. Women were widely used as medics in the Soviet Army and 12 received the ultimate decoration, 'Hero of the Soviet Union' for their brave work.

LEFT: A well-armed partisan leader with his Mosin Model 1891/30 rifle. He also has a belt of German 7.92mm (0.31in) machine-gun ammunition, a German P'08 Luger pistol in its leather holster, a Soviet RGD-33 grenade and a captured map case. Attacks on small German patrols and outposts would enable partisans to restock with ammunition for captured weapons or acquire new ones. Food could be demanded off the local population.

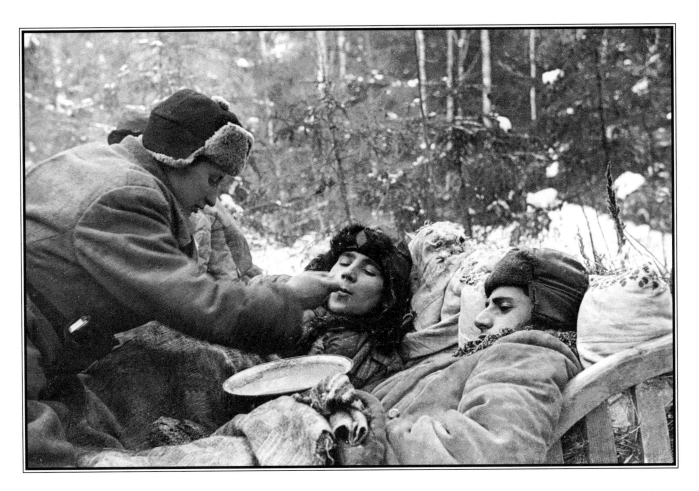

ABOVE: Casualties are hand-fed in the grim setting of a partisan field hospital in the winter. Although some drugs, painkillers and bandages might be available, they would be in very limited supply. Recovery for wounded men and women would have more to do with their physical strength and the severity of their injury. Hospitalisation could be the result of infection, as the swamps and woodland where partisans' bases were established were cold, damp, unhealthy environments.

RIGHT: A rather staged picture of a partisan attack – if it were actual combat, the photographer would seem to be in the line of fire. In a real attack, the partisans would not have chosen to bunch up, putting themselves at risk of destruction by mortar or machine-gun fire. Nor would an experienced group have chosen to go to ground in the middle of an exposed field and return fire – their best move would be to launch as fast and violent an attack as possible on the enemy position. If this were a real attack, the Germans could pick off the partisans one by one.

ABOVE: A partisan group commanded by A. S.Yegorov in the mountains of Lower Tatry. Mountains, like woods and swamps, were ideal terrain for partisans, who could then control the approaches and spot enemy troop movements towards their bases. Basing themselves in these environments would also mean that they knew the escape routes. To ensure that these groups would pose no threat to Moscow when their operational areas were liberated, the partisans were quickly absorbed into the Soviet Army, although some partisan leaders were executed by the NKVD secret police.

LEFT: Partisans, one armed with a Tokarev SVT1938/1940 automatic rifle, gather around a felled telegraph pole in a wood in winter. The men may be booby trapping the pole in order to kill or injure German signals troops who might attempt to re-erect it. The pole may equally have been positioned across a road as a simple obstacle that a German driver would move and so trigger the booby trap. Although the Soviet Army had various booby trap mechanisms, partisans would probably have improvised a device using a hand grenade with a trip or pull wire.

LEFT: Battered after a violent attack by partisans, a German railway security post stands abandoned in Russia on the Korosten-Kalinkovichi railway track in February 1944. The lightly constructed 10m (33ft) high watchtower, with its exposed ladders, would have been a death trap when the position came under a concerted attack. Attacks on fixed positions like this security post could also be used by the partisans to draw more troops into the area and catch them in prepared ambushes at vulnerable points on the railway or roads.

ABOVE: The Commissars and military leaders of a mixed partisan group hold a daylight parade in a village in Belorussia. A parade such as this one, complete with a band, would be held as a political gesture to demonstrate that the partisans were in control of the area and also to attract more recruits. Veterans of the Civil War of 1918–22 who fought with the partisans understood very well the value of demonstrations such as this. In Orel province, about 18,000 partisans controlled an area comprising 490 villages and maintained Soviet rule and administration.

THE BATTLE OF THE RAILWAYS

Railways were a particularly vulnerable target – vital to the German war machine, but with long, exposed stretches that passed through woodland or remote areas.

BELOW: A derailed locomotive lies abandoned – the trucks have been detached and recovered following this partisan attack, which may simply have entailed cutting or even unbolting one length of track. Faced by these attacks, the Germans set up fixed positions covering vulnerable areas and protected them with anti-personnel minefields, shot at civilians who ventured near the track and used empty trains as bait.

RIGHT: Partisans armed with 7.62mm (0.3in) Mosin Nagant M1891/30 bolt-action rifles prepare a railway bridge for demolition. The masonry and steel girder construction would make it a hard target. Even if the charge did not destroy the bridge, however, but only weakened or distorted the structure, this would still mean that trains would have to cross it slowly, imposing delays on the logistic support for the German forces.

RIGHT: A small troop train derailed by partisans commanded by I. U. Ushakov lies abandoned near Pilotiza in Czechoslovakia, in 1944. The lack of damage to the tracks suggests that the engineers of the *Deutsches Reichsbahn* filled in the crater and relaid the tracks, but decided that recovering the rolling stock was impractical – probably for lack of heavy lifting gear. In Belorussia alone, between August and November 1943, the railway lines were cut 200,000 times, 1014 trains were wrecked or derailed, and 72 bridges were destroyed or damaged by partisans. Such disruption inevitably had a serious effect on the logistic supply of the Wehrmacht at the front. Unfortunately for the Germans, there was no real alternative to moving supplies by rail. The Luftwaffe could not airlift all the supplies needed, and the road system was too poor to cope with the heavy volume of traffic required.

LEFT: A guard's van from a German train teeters on the edge of a demolished bridge in western Russia. In the water beneath lie the remains of the rest of the train. The partisans who launched this attack probably linked a charge to a pressure switch or an anti-tank mine so that, as the train passed over the bridge, it detonated the explosives. Bridges were prime targets for partisan attack and were therefore guarded and inspected. Hence the charges which destroyed this bridge would have been skilfully concealed.

ABOVE: A recovery problem beyond the resources of the German railway engineers, a locomotive and tender lie derailed by the trackside. Destroying locomotives was a far more effective tactic than destroying rolling stock, which could be more easily replaced. However, for the Germans, once the Soviet railway gauge had been converted from broad to standard, there was the whole of occupied Europe which could be called on to provide more locomotives and stock as replacements.

LEFT: German rolling stock burns after an attack by Soviet Partisans in western Russia. Incendiary devices could be manufactured from items readily available from domestic sources and simple timers like a candle or a smouldering cigarette attached. If the target that was selected was either explosive or inflammable an attack could be devastating. For German soldiers these attacks were often unpredictable and unnerving and made the whole population, including women and children, appear to be potential enemies.

RIGHT: The original caption describes these men as Romanians who were students of a Special Force School of the Ukrainian Partisan Movements Headquarters. While Romania did eventually join the Soviet Union and attack its erstwhile ally Germany, it is more probable that these men are Soviet partisans in training. They have dug out ballast from under the track and are positioning a charge made up of slab explosives. This will either cut the track or buckle it badly and will probably derail a train. Sentries have taken position further down the track to protect the demolition team.

BELOW: A German troop train in the western Soviet Union which was derailed by Ukrainian partisans in Czerny Zag, in December 1944. Soviet railways were broad gauge and so, immediately after the invasion in 1941, German engineers had to lift the track and convert it to standard European gauge in order to allow the *Deutsches Reichsbahn* rolling stock to operate in Russia. Railways were a far more effective way of transporting men and equipment than road or air, and so partisans made them a priority target for sabotage attacks in what was to become known as the 'Battle of the Railways'.

ABOVE: A German-occupied building in Russia burns as a Soviet partisan team watches under cover. This picture was probably posed, as the partisans are well lit and it is very unlikely that they would remain in the area after an incendiary attack had taken place. In reality, they would escape quickly as soon as the fuse had been lit and might perhaps return at dawn in the guise of an innocent peasant to undertake an after-action reconnaissance of the target.

LEFT: Horsemen in the wheat fields – a mounted partisan reconnaissance patrol uses the cover of the standing crop to observe. Horses were an ideal mode of transport for the partisans. The animals required only water and fodder, and were therefore a low maintenance and very flexible means of getting about. In an emergency, they could even be slaughtered for food. Experienced riders learned to secure their horses either in a hollow or with their heads towards the enemy, so that the swishing movement of their tails would not attract attention.

LEFT: A partisan Pulemet Degtyareva Pekhotnii (DP) light machine-gun crew support an assault. The gun, designed in the 1920s by Vasily Alexeyevich Degtyarev, was a simple gas-operated weapon with only six moving parts. It had been adopted by the Soviet Army in 1928 following two years of trials. Despite these trials, during the war the DP was revealed to have a return spring which weakened after sustained periods of firing and a bipod which had a tendency to buckle when the gun was placed heavily in position.

RIGHT: Here, partisans creep forwards during an attack on a timber bridge that they have selected for demolition. The more important the bridge, the more likely it would have a heavy German presence to defend it. Although attacks on targets such as bridges would inconvenience the Germans and reduce their mobility and logistics traffic, they would also cause problems for the local population. German reprisals, as well as local hostility, often made partisan operations difficult in some areas of the Ukraine which had never been overjoyed at the prospect of Communist rule. When the Germans began to retreat in the autumn of 1943, large elements of the population moved with them, knowing that they would be victimised by the Soviet secret police, the NKVD, after the Red Army had liberated the area.

RIGHT: Wearing an officer's *kozhanoe snaryazhenie* (Sam Browne belt), with its distinctive star-shaped buckle, and a low-crowned kubanka black fleece cap, A. G. Kondratuk looks more like a regular officer in the Soviet Army than the commander of an active partisan group. Kondratuk headed the 2nd Stalin Vinnytsya Partisan Brigade based in the Kiev area of the Ukraine in the winter of 1944, when the war was clearly in the Soviet's favour. Within a partisan group, these external accoutrements would help to distinguish the leader and enhance his public standing. The brigade would fight alongside the regular Red Army while the Germans were pushed out of the Ukraine.

BELOW:. The 'Stalin' Czech Communist partisan group commanded by M. I. Shukaev in December 1944, operating in the forests of Cerniy Zag in eastern Czechoslovakia. The partisan and resistance groups survived in inhospitable or inaccessible areas such as forests, swamps or mountains, which offered cover and escape routes. One of the prices they paid for this security was having to endure bitter winters in the open and the plagues of insects in the summer months. In such inaccessible areas the groups' lack of heavy weapons was not the disadvantage it would normally be. German measures against partisans could be brutal and arbitrary. Caught in the middle was the terrorised civilian population.

RIGHT: Partisans in the Leningrad area open fire with an 82-PM 36 82mm (3.22in) mortar on 23 February 1944. This 62kg (136.7lb) weapon fired a 3.4kg (7.5lb) or 3.35kg (7.39lb) bomb to a maximum range of 3000m (3280yds). It could also fire German 81mm (3.18in) ammunition, although less accurately. This made it an ideal weapon for partisans, who could restock from captured supplies. A well-trained crew could put 25 rounds into the air in a minute – in the snow, this crew would be slower and the base plate may well settle and so make the mortar less accurate.

BELOW: M. A. Doronovskayaa, a female partisan radio operator, with her assistant A. G. Semenova, receives instructions from Moscow in 1944. For Stalin's government, these radio links with the partisans were normally provided by trained operators who had been parachuted into the area, as well as NKVD officers who had arrived the same way. This tactic provided the government with a degree of control over these autonomous groups. After they had been liberated, many former partisans were immediately drafted into the Soviet Army to ensure the break-up of the groups.

CHAPTER EIGHT

Red Winter

An Unstoppable Offensive

Between August and December 1943, the Soviet Army in the Ukraine and Belorussia rolled onto an unstoppable offensive. On 5 August, Kharkov was finally liberated (for the last time) by the Steppe Front and, on 25 September, Russian forces recaptured Smolensk and, later, Bryansk. In October, the Kuban bridgehead opposite the Crimea was eliminated and this effectively closed the Sea of Azov to German shipping. A month later, Dneproptrovsk was liberated and, on 6 November, a devastated Kiev, the Ukrainian capital, was recaptured by the Voronezh Front. The city was taken in a day by General Vatutin's forces because the bulk of the German forces had been allowed to withdraw by Hitler to stronger positions on the Dniepr bend.

WINTER TACTICS

The Red Army had always been expert at winter operations and exploiting the severe conditions, and so, following the muddy autumn season, it was back onto the offensive against the Germans still on Soviet soil. On 19 January 1944, the ancient city of Novgorod was liberated. A week later, the long-running siege of Leningrad was finally broken by the Red Army, as German forces were driven out of artillery range. The city had been almost completely cut off for 900 days and, during this time, about one million of its inhabitants had died from disease, starvation and enemy action. The Soviet offensive around Leningrad did not halt until early March, by which time it had reached the Narva-Lake Peipus–Vitebsk line.

In February, 60,000 men, elements of six German divisions, were trapped in the pocket caused by attacks by the 1st Ukrainian Front under General Vatutin from the Kiev

LEFT: Russian Naval Aviation armourers of the Black Sea Fleet manoeuvre a 940kg (2072lb) torpedo towards an Ilyushin DB-PT torpedo bomber in 1943.

FAR LEFT: I. V. Bocharova, a female armourer of the Soviet Air Force, loads the 12.7mm (0.5in) Berezin UB machine gun in the upper cowling of a Yakovlev Yak-9D fighter.

bridgehead and the 2nd Ukrainian Front under Marshal Koniev from the Cherkassy bridgehead. Attacks by the 3rd and 47th Panzer Corps broke through to the Cherkassy pocket to relieve those surrounded by the Soviet forces, but only 30,000 men managed to escape.

GRABBING HUNGARY

On 20 March, in *Unternehmen Margaretha* (Operation Margaretha), German forces occupied the territory of their wavering Axis partner Hungary to ensure that it remained in the war. Not only was it vital for the Germans to keep Hungarian troops in the front line on the Eastern Front, but also the oil from Hungary's modest deposits was essential for the Germans' war effort.

Finland, who had sided with Germany in 1941 during Operation Barbarossa and had recaptured the territory lost to the Soviet Union in the Winter War between 1939 and 1940, had fought a largely defensive war once their aims had been achieved, much to the annoyance of their German allies. In June 1944, with German forces pulling back towards the Reich and out of direct contact with the Finnish army, a Soviet offensive broke through the Finnish defences and, on 4 September 1944, the President of Finland, Field Marshal Carl Gustav Mannerheim, signed an armistice with the Soviet Union and declared war on Germany.

BELOW: A PzKpfw IV Ausf G drives towards Kharkov, following a signpost put up by the *Feldpolizei* (Military Police). At Hitler's insistence, the tank's short 75mm (2.95in) gun was replaced by a long KwK 40 L/43 gun. Armoured plates known as *schürzen* (skirts) were added to later marks to protect the tank's thinner armour behind the wheels from close-range anti-tank weapons. This spaced armour was also fitted to the turret to protect against hollow-charge weapons. When the Germans introduced the Haft-Hohlladung 3kg (6.6lb), a hand-emplaced magnetic shaped anti-tank charge, they coated their tanks' hulls with *Zimmerit*, a cement which prevented these charges from adhering, so captured examples could not be used against them.

LEFT: Uncrated bombs stacked with characteristic Russian insouciance on the edge of an airfield operating Petlyakov Pe-2 dive-bombers. The Pe-2 was a demanding aircraft for its pilot to fly, but it equipped several élite Guards regiments. The most remarkable was the 125th M. M. Raskova Borisov Guards Bomber Regiment, the air and ground crew of which were all women. Between 1943 and 1945, the regiment flew 1134 sorties, with some crews flying three sorties a day, and dropped 980,000kg (2,160,530lbs) of bombs. These fast turn-arounds between sorties were as quick as anything that the Luftwaffe had managed to deliver in all their close-support operations for frontline troops in 1940–43.

LEFT: Soviet sappers dash forwards to extinguish a fire in buildings in Kharkov in the Ukraine following its liberation in August 1943. In all armies in World War II, sappers were called upon to perform a multitude of tasks from mine laying and demolitions to the construction of bunkers and fortifications, and the rebuilding of demolished infrastructure such as bridges, power stations and reservoirs. Unlike their counterparts in the West, Soviet sappers did not have heavy construction plant.

RIGHT: Soviet soldiers armed with PPSh-41 submachine guns move inland after crossing the River Dniepr in the summer of 1943. By 1945, some 5,000,00 Pistolet-Pulemet Shpagina o1941g or PPSh-41 had been produced. The gun designed by G. S. Shpagin weighed 3.5kg (7.7lbs) and used two barrels from a Mosin Nagant M1891/30 rifles which were chromed to reduce corrosion and wear. The drum magazine held 71 rounds.

ABOVE: Dressed in *mochalniy*-hooded camouflaged suits, a section of Soviet soldiers races past a knocked-out 75mm (2.95in) Panzerjäger 38 (t) Marder III in August 1943. Only 418 of these interim self-propelled anti-tank guns were produced by marrying a 75mm (2.95in) Pak 40 anti-tank gun with the chassis of an ex-Czech Praga TNH/LT38 tank. The man standing on the left by the vehicle suggests that the photograph was posed and the smoke is from a grenade or burning tyre.

LEFT: An abandoned German 75mm (2.95in) Pak 97/38.L/36.3 anti-tank gun in Novosibirsk, following its liberation in September 1943. The gun has been skilfully sited among the ruins, which give added protection and would make it hard to detect. The 75mm Pak was a combination of a captured French M1897 75mm (2.95in) gun barrel on a Pak 38 carriage. The barrel was strengthened and fitted with perforated Solothurn muzzle brake, and could penetrate 60mm (2.46in) of armour at 900m (984yds).

LEFT: Balancing his PPSh-41 submachine gun on its drum magazine, a Soviet soldier covers his comrades as they race across open ground towards a distant village in the autumn of 1943. The photograph appears carefully posed – the PPSh-41 fired a 7.62mm (0.3in) pistol calibre round that would not be effective against targets in the distant buildings and this weapon has the simple short-range flip sight. Finally, the dead German soldier in the foreground seem to have been strategically positioned to complete the picture. All sides were adept at using propaganda to support their cause. By this stage of the war, however, the faked Soviet victories now represented reality on the battlefield, in sharp contrast to their predecessors from 1941 and 1942.

RIGHT: On a chill day, with the captain like a figurehead on the conning tower, a submarine of the Black Sea Fleet conducts long-range gunnery practice with its 100mm gun (3.94in) in 1943. Most of the submarines in the fleet were comparatively modern, having been completed between 1931 and 1937. They were capable of 15 knots on the surface and eight submerged. Some of the boats had fine revolutionary names such as *Revolutioner*, *Spartakovetz* and, rather incongruously, *Chartist*, after the British political movement.

ABOVE: Soviet soldiers of the newly established 1st Ukrainian Front, formerly the Voronezh Front, crossing the River Dniepr on a pontoon bridge during the fighting for Kiev in the autumn of 1943. Earlier, in a race to cut off the men of Army Group South, who were recoiling after the disaster of Kursk, the Soviet forces had crossed the river on rafts, small boats and even inflated vehicle tyre inner tubes. The generals commanding Soviet forces were given their head by Stalin, at precisely the same time as Hitler was determinedly restricting tactical flexibility for his commanders.

RIGHT: Smoke rises from burning buildings south of Lake Ladoga, near Leningrad, on 12 October 1943, as a German *Feldgendarmerie* (Army Military Policeman) stands on duty by a railway crossing. He wears the distinctive cuff title and arm badge of his formation on his left arm and has the metal *Rinkragen* (gorget), with its luminous lettering, around his neck. The Army Military Policemen were responsible for discipline and so were not popular with ordinary German soldiers – the *Rinkragen* earned them the nickname 'Chained Dogs'.

RIGHT: Soviet engineers operating a ferry across the River Severskiy Donetz, near the town of Izum in the Kharkov area, in 1943. On the raft under tow is a T-34/85 tank, distinguishable by the long barrel of the 85mm (3.34in) gun and larger turret. The turret could accommodate three men, so allowing the commander to concentrate on his proper role of fighting the battle.

LEFT: Soldiers from the company commanded by Major V. T. Krudnikov skirmish through a built-up area during the fighting for the Darnitza ridge on the left bank of the River Dniepr near Kiev, in 1943. The PPSh-41 submachine gunner in the foreground may not be a marksman picking his targets, but the volume of fire from a group of men all similarly armed would be awesome and would force an enemy to keep his head down long enough for the Soviet soldiers to reach their objective.

RIGHT: A captured German PzKpfw VI Tiger Ausf E in the Ukraine in 1943. This formidable tank mounted the 88mm (3.46in) KwK 36 gun with 92 rounds of high-explosive or armour-piercing capped, ballistic capped (APCBC) ammunition. The Tiger had none of the sloping angles of the Panther or Tiger II, but it made up for some of these design flaws through sheer strength. The thinnest armour on the Tiger was 26mm (1.02in), while the thickest in the most vulnerable areas was 110mm (4.33in).

ABOVE: A group of Soviet artillery officers confer during a break in the Ukraine, in 1943. Behind them the crews of a 132mm (5.20in) *Katyusha* (Little Katy) rocket battery lounge on US-supplied 6 x 4 Studebaker 2¹/₂-ton trucks fitted with M13 16-rail launchers. On the right, another invaluable US-supplied vehicle, the ¹/₄-ton 4 x 4 Command Reconnaissance (Willys MA) Jeep, approaches the group. The Soviet Union received the majority of the 1500 of these vehicles that were built.

RIGHT: In the cover of a wrecked building on the outskirts of Kiev in 1943, a Soviet Maxim 1910 machine-gun crew engages German positions at long range. The Maxim 1910 remained in production until 1950 and was then passed on to allies of the Soviet Union and liberation armies in the Third World. The gun fired from a 250-round cloth belt at the comparatively slow rate of 550rpm. However, this slow rate of fire, the cooling water jacket and the rugged design of the weapon meant that it was not prone to overheating and therefore did not suffer from jams or malfunctions in action.

LIVING UNDER THE JACKBOOT

German repression bred Soviet resistance and, in turn, partisan attacks prompted further repression in a brutal cycle which only ended with liberation.

BELOW: A curious and rather ghoulish group of German soldiers escort the partisan Zoia Kosmodemianskaia to the gallows. Just before her execution, the Komsomol member turned to them and said, 'You can't hang all 190 million of us.' Two weeks later, during the Soviet counteroffensive, Lidin, a *Pravda* war reporter, found the sequence of photographs and then photographed Kosmodemianskaia's body, which had been recovered still with the noose in place. His account of her execution turned her into a symbol of Soviet resistance and a partisan heroine.

RIGHT: The last moments of Komsomol member Zoia Kosmodemianskaia, hanged by the Germans on 29 November 1941. The Germans have hung a sign reading 'She set fire to houses' around her neck. This was a common practice intended to explain why the sentence had been carried out. Kosmodemianskaia was caught while she attempted to set fire to stables housing German Army horses in the village of Petrischevo. Under brutal interrogation, she revealed no information and so, as was common practice with captured partisans, the Germans hanged her.

LEFT: Women and children crowd onto crudely camouflaged railway flat cars during the evacuation of the Ukraine in 1941. Not all the civilians in the fiercely independent Ukraine would see the Germans as invaders – in fact, many regarded them as liberators and welcomed them as men who would free the population from Stalin's ruthless control. As well as evacuating civilians, the Soviet government dismantled industrial plant and shipped it to new factory sites beyond the Urals and out of range of Luftwaffe bombers.

BELOW: In the 1920s, the Don Cossacks had suffered under Stalin, persecuted as property-owning *kulaks*. In Russia during World War II, the German Field Marshal Paul Ludwig Ewald von Kleist formed good relations with minority groups and was able to recruit central Asians and Cossacks to fight for the Germans. Enough Cossacks volunteered to serve in the German armed forces to make up RONA, the 15th Cossack Cavalry Corps. In this photograph, a small group of Don Cossacks bearing a Swastika flag as their colours parades through a Russian village.

LEFT: Flanked by the remains of a village that has been burned to the ground, a partisan group walks casually down the central road. The partisan war was particularly brutal and the mass execution of hostages and destruction of villages was common practice. It was prompted by an urge for revenge and in an attempt to cow the population into tacit support for the German occupiers. Sometimes these tactics were successful, but sometimes they became a very effective recruiting campaign for the partisans, as men and women craved revenge for these excesses.

BELOW: Russian women laden with a few personal possessions plod back to their village along a track rutted by tanks and trucks following the end of fighting in the Kharkov area in 1943. They look surprisingly cheerful given the circumstances, but this may simply be the face of relief. Tragically, often all that remained of the wooden homes they returned to was the brick chimneys. The women are wearing the traditional Orenburg scarf, made from a very warm, light wool similar to cashmere.

ABOVE: The surviving population of a Ukrainian village, largely made up of the young, female or very old, greets a column of T-34/76D tanks as it drives through in the summer of 1943. The huge losses in manpower suffered by the Soviet Union in World War II meant that, in the 1950s and early 1960s, many heavy manual jobs such as construction work, heavy industry and farming which would fomerly have been carried out by men were perforce undertaken by women.

LEFT: Huddled against the cold, refugees return by sledge to the village of Adjanka, in the Kirovgrad region of the Ukraine, following its liberation in the winter of 1944. By this stage of the war, grim though conditions were, for these civilians there was at least the knowledge that the Soviet Union was on the offensive and that German forces would be unlikely to counterattack through their villages and farms. Somewhat miraculously, they have been able to retain their horses – neither the Soviet Army nor the German has seized them for transport or food.

LEFT: Tank riders of the 1st Ukrainian Front huddle aboard a T-34 as it advances down Krasnoarmeyskaya Street in the city centre of Kiev, following its liberation on 6 November 1943. Engine heat would make the rear deck a warm perch for the soldiers at the onset of winter. The Kiev population had suffered cruelly under a long and brutal German occupation. It was common practice for groups of randomly selected hostages to be shot if acts of even minor resistance or sabotage were detected.

RIGHT: Soldiers from a platoon commanded by Sergeant Vinograd fighting through the suburbs of Kiev in 1943. When the ancient city was liberated by the troops of General Nikolai Vatutin's 1st Ukrainian Front, they discovered that it had been deliberately devastated and that its art treasures had been looted and shipped to Germany. These thefts were part of a policy of amassing art treasures in the Reich which was directed by Alfred Rosenberg, Reich Minister for the Occupied Eastern Territories.

RIGHT: T-34/76D tanks of the 3rd Guards Tank Army of the 1st Ukrainian Front parked in a concentration area at the edge of the Puscha-Voditza woods on the outskirts of Kiev, on 5 November 1943. The 3rd Guards Tank Army had driven north from Bukrin on the River Dniepr and punched through the German defences to the north of Kiev, before swinging south and east to trap the Hessian 88th Infantry Division in a pocket in the city. Kiev was liberated on 6 November and a huge bridgehead opened up across the Dniepr. Six days after Kiev, Zhitomir fell to a joint assault by the Belorussian and 1st Ukrainian Fronts; however, a counterattack by the XLVIII Panzer Corps against the Kiev bridgehead recaptured the city.

ABOVE: Horses and riders of the 1st Guards Cavalry Corps cross a timber bridge over the River Dniepr during the battle for Kiev on 5 November 1943. Cavalry were not recruited exclusively from the Don and Ukraine, but also from areas of Soviet Central Asia where there was a strong tradition of horsemanship. There were five Uzbeki, three Tadzhik, three Kirkhiz, two Turkmen, twelve Kazakh, two Kalmyk, two Bakshir, one Checheno-Ingush and one Kabardino-Balkarian cavalry divisions.

BELOW: Geysers of smoke, dirt and water rise above the River Dniepr in autumn 1943, as German shells burst near Soviet boats. Although shells might not score direct hits, the waves from an explosion might be sufficient to upset an overcrowded boat. To troops given the task of an assault river crossing, the expanse of water could look doubly daunting – with no cover, it was exposed to direct and indirect fire, and, if the enemy did not kill you, there was always the prospect of drowning.

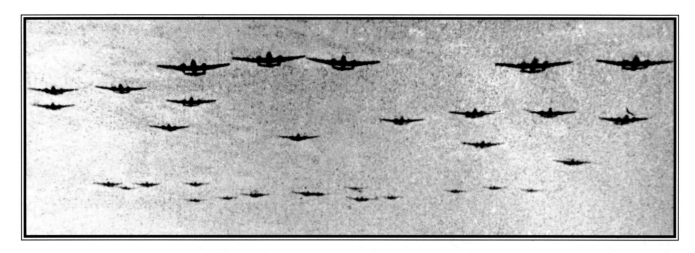

ABOVE: Tight formations of Petlyakov Pe-2 bombers en route to attack a target near Kiev in 1943. By the close of the war, Soviet aircraft factories had built 11,427 Pe-2 bombers. They saw action in Manchuria in the fast moving Soviet invasion in 1945. After the war, they equipped several Soviet satellite air forces. The ground-attack version, the Pe-2Sh, had a formidable armament of two ventral 20mm ((0.79in) Sh VAK cannon and two 12.7mm (0.5in) UBS heavy machine guns.

RIGHT: A loose formation of Petlyakov Pe-2 bombers en route to neutralise enemy positions in support of the 1st Ukrainian Front attacking Kiev. The Pe-2 had a maximum speed about half that of the British de Havilland Mosquito, but in many ways the aircraft are similar, as both were configured in different marks as fast bombers, fighters and as reconnaissance aircraft.

LEFT: Two officers of the 1st Ukrainian Front, in the foreground, watch the distant effects of an artillery bombardment during the fighting around Kiev in 1943. The temporary positions dug rapidly beside a track are typical of the way in which, whenever Soviet soldiers halted in the forward areas, they would dig in. Each man carried a short entrenching tool and was trained to dig in with it from a prone position. This short spade was often sharpened and also used in close combat as a hand axe, similar to the way entrenching tools were used as weapons in the trenches of World War I.

LEFT: Soldiers sprint up the left bank of the River Dniepr in an assault river crossing. This photograph is probably a rehearsal exercise or staged after the event, as the lack of casualties and the fact that the photographer has stopped on a hostile shore – apparently under artillery fire – to take the picture is either insanely brave or foolishly reckless. What the photograph does convey, however, is how critical it is to move forwards as fast as possible from a beach or river bank, as enemy artillery will know the range of these targets to a metre.

BELOW: Soviet soldiers of the 1st Ukrainian Front hug the ground as an artillery barrage explodes around them during the fighting for Kiev. Infantry in the open were terribly vulnerable under artillery fire, but even armoured vehicles could be damaged. A heavy barrage would force the crew to close their hatches, reducing visibility. Direct hits on a tank could damage optical equipment and radio antennae. However, small fragments that would do little harm to a tank could kill or injure a foot soldier. This puts into context the insane courage of Soviet tank-riding infantry.

LEFT: The formidable obstacle presented by a major river in Russia is well illustrated by the bridge across the River Dniepr constructed by the regiment of engineers commanded by Colonel I. U. Barenboim in 1943. The timber piers in the river must not only bear the weight of trucks and tanks, but also be strong enough to withstand the battering from ice flows in the winter and the fast current generated during the spring thaw which will be carrying trees and other flotsam.

BELOW: Marshal of the Soviet Union Georgi Konstantinovich Zhukov addressing troops and the population following the liberation of Kiev in November 1943. Zhukov stands out as one of the finest leaders of the Soviet Army, fighting and winning defensive battles at Moscow and Leningrad, then moving onto the offensive at Stalingrad and Kursk, and leading his troops to victory in Berlin in 1945. From an NCO in the Imperial Russian Army, he rose to be the Soviet Minister of Defence after the war.

RIGHT: Fireworks in Moscow, the Russian capital, celebrate the liberation of Kiev, the Ukrainian capital. For the citizens of the capital of the Soviet Union, life had been grim without exception for nearly three years and, for Stalin and the Communist Party, the liberation presented an ideal opportunity to 'pat them on the back'. Stalin had realised that the most effective appeal to the population was to present the war as patriotic and not as a clash between two political ideologies. The Army received new uniforms, special medals and a ranking structure was reintroduced.

RIGHT: An armoured train with turrets traversed ready to go into action. The distinctive silhouette of a 12.7mm (0.5in) Degtyarev Shpagin DShK M1938 heavy machine gun fitted with an AA sight can be seen to the right. The DShK was a gas-operated, air-cooled machine gun which fired a 50-round belt. It had an effective range of 1500m (1640yds) and, in the AA role, of 1000m (1094yds). In the ground role, it was mounted on a wheeled carriage. The gun was first produced in 1934 in limited numbers and revised in 1938 (the DShK M1938). After the war, it was once again revised and the feed mechanism improved. It remained in production until 1980 and is still widely used throughout the world.

LEFT: This photograph of T-34/76D tanks advancing across ground frozen solid in a hard frost in 1943 shows the low silhouette and well-angled armour of these excellent tanks. The big road wheels of the US-designed Christie suspension were less likely to jam with mud and dirt than the German tanks, which had small road wheels and return rollers above them for the track. The German suspension system also left the side of the hull exposed to hits by anti-tank weapons.

RIGHT: The driver of a *Samochodnaya Ustanovka* self-propelled SU122 Assault Howitzer drives carefully across a pontoon bridge over the River Dniepr. The SU122 had angled 20mm (0.79in) to 45mm (1.77in) armour and used the engine and chassis of a T-34/76. Its role was to provide direct gunfire support. Firing high-explosive anti-tank (HEAT) rounds, it could penetrate 200mm (7.87in) of armour at 630m (689yds); with a high-explosive (HE) round, it could reach out to 11,800m (12,905yds). The wide T-34 tracks gave the SU122 a low ground pressure and thus allowed it to manoeuvre across mud and soft snow. Commonality of engine parts with the tank also made for savings in logistics and spares. German tanks such as the PzKpfw III and IV had to have special extensions fitted to their tracks to spread the weight.

LEFT: The pilots of the Soviet Air Force 146th Independent Fighter Regiment rest on one knee while receiving their regimental Guards colours at a ceremony at Bovary, a town which has now become a suburb of Kiev, in the winter of 1943. As befits an élite fighter formation, the single-seat Yakovlev Yak-9 long-range fighters lined up behind the pilots have a spectacular tail fin insignia of a red star with the lines of a red and yellow sunburst radiating from it.

RIGHT: Anti-tank gunners of the Voronezh Front move their 45mm (1.77in) Model 1932 L/46 gun near Kharkov in the winter of 1943. The Model 1932 weighed 510kg (1124lbs) in action and fired a 1.43kg (3.15lb) shell that was capable of penetrating 38mm (1.50in) of armour at an angle of 30 degrees at a range of 1000m (1094yds). It remained in service throughout the war. The gun was based on the German 37mm (1.46in) Rheinmetall Pak 35/36 L/45 anti-tank gun. The Germans designated captured guns as 45mm (1.77in) Pak 184(r).

ABOVE: Whitewashed T-34/76D tanks of 1st Ukrainian Front pulled over on the side of the Zhitomir Shosse, a highway on the outskirts of Kiev, in December 1943. A distinctive feature of the T-34 and all Soviet tanks were the wide tracks that spread the weight over a larger area and allowed these vehicles to cross snow and soft ground. The tanks have been brought forwards to repel an attack by the well-equipped, experienced XLVIII Panzer Corps, which forced them back from Zhitomir, which was briefly recaptured by the Germans. However it proved to be a temporary success for the Wehrmacht.

RIGHT: A DShK 1938 heavy machine gunner dug in to cover on road on the outskirts of Zhitomir in the Ukraine in December 1943. The soldier is armed with a rifle for personal protection, as the machine gun would be too bulky to handle if an enemy managed to get close to the weapons pit. On the road, a US-supplied Studebaker 2^1/$_2$-ton 6 x 4 truck tows a 76.2mm (3.0in) M1943/SIS 3 (76-42) field gun past a convoy of tanks. US vehicles were critical in Soviet mobile operations after 1943.

LEFT: Soviet troops, some dressed in white snow camouflage uniforms, dismount from a train to launch a localised attack in the winter of 1942–43. The train appears to be a conventional goods train fitted with AA guns and improvised protection. In winter, the wind chill on these exposed positions would be cruel even for troops as tough and well equipped as Soviet soldiers. The train would probably have been moving men and equipment forwards and not employed as an armoured train, as in the early years of the war in the East.

BELOW:. Two German GW II fuer 105mm (4.13in) le FH 18/1 Wespe (Wasp) self-propelled guns – the one in the foreground named 'Annelliese' by its five-man crew – stand abandoned in the Ukraine in 1943. The Wespe combined the 105mm (4.13in) le FH howitzer with the chassis of the PzKpfw II. It was not an ideal vehicle as the crew in the fighting compartment were unprotected on top and to the rear, and so vulnerable to the elements, as well as counter battery fire.

LEFT: Two whitewashed PzKpfw IV Ausf G tanks in the winter of 1943. The German tanks have spare track links attached to their glacis plates, as well as *schürzen* side armour plates for protection. The Ausf G was distinguishable from the Ausf F by the double-baffle muzzle brake on its 75mm ((2.95in) KwK 40 L/43 gun.

BELOW: Another view of the two snow camouflaged German PzKpfw IV Ausf G tanks knocked out in the winter of 1943 by troops of the 1st Ukrainian Front. The tank in the foreground has spare running wheels in a rack welded to the hull side. In the event of mine damage, this allowed the crew to undertake simple repairs.

RIGHT: Soldiers of the Soviet 6th Army of Lieutenant General Malinovsky's South-West Front are caught in fighting in the winter of 1943. Using the banks of snow cleared from the railway lines as cover, they advance towards a building to drive out the German defenders. The Soviet offensive during the winter of 1943, continuing on from the one that followed the German attack at Kursk in the autumn, allowed the Wehrmacht defenders no respite to regroup and prepare a structured defence. They could do nothing but wait for the spring thaw, which would bring mud in such quantities that even the Soviets' rate of progress would be slowed to nothing more than a crawl.

ABOVE: One of more than 2000 Lisunov Li-2 transport aircraft, the Soviet licence-built version of the US Douglas DC-3 Dakota, is unloaded near Millerrov in 1943. The Soviet Air Force had received 709 DC-3s as Lend Lease Aid before the Soviet Union started licence production. The Li-2 was fitted with a turret in the upper and two positions in the aft fuselage for defensive armament. It could carry 4536kg (10,000lbs) of cargo or 28 troops or 18 litters. Soviet aircraft were fitted with skis in place of the wheeled undercarriage for operations in deep snow, which gave the Red Air Force added operational flexibility.

RIGHT: A Soviet patrol of the 1st Baltic Front in the snow in the winter of 1943. Here, the men support the cold metal of the magazines of their PPSh-41 submachine guns with their left mitt–protected left hands. The group is quite closely bunched – this may be for the benefit of the photographer, as it would otherwise make them vulnerable to automatic weapons, mortar or shell fire. At night, however, it is easier for a commander to communicate with and control a small patrol which remains close together. Instructions can be whispered or even sent by touch.

LEFT: German troops move down a track past two knocked-out Soviet T-34/76B tanks near the town of Nevel in the Pskov region, on 30 December 1943. The crews of the two tanks appear to have overestimated the cross-country capability of the tanks. The front vehicle has come off its track and bogged in the soft ground and the rear vehicle, attempting to manoeuvre past it, has suffered the same fate – faced with the prospect of death or capture, the tank crews have sensibly chosen to bale out.

BELOW: The tarpaulin covers have been removed to show this Soviet T-34/76E tank distinction from earlier marks with its commander's cupola. The tank had thicker turret armour and a new five-speed transmission, as well as more extensive welding and mechanical improvements. This T-34/76E here is one of many loaded onto a railway flat car and crossing a newly rebuilt bridge in 1943 en route to re-equip armoured divisions fighting in the Ukraine or Belorussia. The effectiveness of tarpaulins as concealment can be seen by the anonymous shapes on the other cars.

LEFT: Soviet soldiers in snow camouflage move off from a column of *Lyokhy Tank* T-70 light tanks. The T-70 entered service in January 1942; it had a crew of two and was armed with a 45mm (1.77in) gun with 70 rounds and a 7.62mm (0.3in) DT machine gun. The tank was made at the Gorki Automobile Works and, when production ceased in 1943, they had built 8226 vehicles. Despite the T-70's narrow tracks, its weight of 9960kg (21,958lbs) meant that drivers were able to take it across firm snow.

BELOW: Under a light guard, a long column of German prisoners captured in the Korsun-Shevchenkovskiy battle in the Kiev region in January 1944 plods across a bridge in western Russia. Shocked and exhausted after capture, the best chance of survival for soldiers in hostile territory in winter was to remain part of a large group of prisoners. Escape, unless friendly forces were very close, was an option that held very little hope. German prisoners were used on heavy reconstruction work and eventually returned from the Soviet Union in the mid-1950s.

RIGHT: Smoke pours from a PzKpfw IV, as a group of Soviet infantry follow a T-34/76D of the 3rd Guards Tank Army of the 1st Ukrainian Front in January 1944. The officer standing on the hull of the T-34 makes this photograph rather unconvincing as an 'action' shot showing the events as they happened. If the infantry needed to climb onto the hull to talk to tank crews, it was wiser and safer to squat close to the turret for protection, while the commander looked out from behind the cover of his hatch.

BELOW: Soviet officers dressed in *bekesha* (fur-lined overcoats) and *polushubok* (short sheepskin coats) watch at a safe distance during the Korsun-Shevchenkovskiy battle in the winter of 1944, as with their distinctive shriek 132mm (5.20in) *Katyusha* (Little Katy) rockets streak away from their truck-mounted M13 16-rail rocket launcher. The rockets were not a precision weapon, but precision was hardly necessary if 16 impacted in an area about the size of four football pitches and dumped nearly 300kg (660lbs) of explosives on the target – the whistle of the rockets' approach was much feared by the Germans.

ABOVE: A loose formation of Soviet Air Force Ilyushin Il-2m3 *Shturmoviki* aircraft of the 3rd Ukrainian Front in February 1944. The Il-2 that proved formidable as a ground-attack aircraft had originally been designed as a fighter. The two-seater version was armed with two fixed forward firing 23mm (0.9in) VYa cannon in the wings, two 7.62mm (0.3in) ShKAS machine guns in the fuselage and a flexible 12.7 UBT machine gun in the rear. It could carry up to 600kg (1323lbs) of external ordnance.

LEFT: Waves of Soviet infantry move forwards against a distant German position in the Korsun-Shevchenkovskiy battle in the Kiev region February 1944. This looks like an authentic action picture from the Eastern Front. For German soldiers in Russia, the almost suicidal Soviet attacks were terrifying. The Soviet infantry were charged with a mixture of patriotic and political fervour, and this was topped off with several slugs of strong vodka. They then advanced, often with arms linked, cheering with a distinctive thundering shout of 'Oorah! Oorah!'

RIGHT: A knocked-out German PzKpfw IV Ausf F2 with the distinctive ball-shaped muzzle brake on its long KwK 40 L/43 gun in a vehicle graveyard in the Korsun-Shevchenkovskiy battle in the Kiev in the winter of 1944. This up-gunned version of the PzKpfw IV appeared in March 1942 as an answer to the T-34. The gun was capable of penetrating 77mm (3.03in) of homogeneous armour at 2000m (2187yds) and the tank carried 87 rounds of four different types of ammunition.

BELOW: A litter of German vehicles with a PzKpfw IV Ausf F2 tank on 23 February 1944, in the Korsun-Shevchenkovskiy battle near Kiev. The mixture of horse-drawn and wheeled vehicles suggests that this may have been a convoy, evading Soviet armour, with the single tank as escort. Silhouetted against the snow, they would have been easy pickings for roaming Soviet tanks. With a lack of fresh meat in midwinter, the horse carcasses have been removed from the vehicles as rations.

LEFT: A German PzKpfw IV Ausf F2 in the Korsun-Shevchenkovskiy pocket jammed against a horse-drawn small field kitchen, distinguishable by its chimney, on 23 February 1944. The field kitchen was drawn by two or four horses and consisted of a limber and trailer – the former for rations, cooking utensils and to carry the cookhouse staff, the latter with a solid fuel oven. It was capable of feeding 50 to 150 men. Stews were easy to cook and could be distributed to frontline units in insulated containers that could be man-packed.

BELOW: Burned, blasted and abandoned German transport litters a vast track across the steppe on 23 February 1944, after an attack by the Soviet Air Force. For Soviet ground-attack aircraft, notably the heavily armoured Il-2, the soft-skinned vehicles were an easy prey as they attempted to escape westwards through the snow. The churned and muddy track past the village on the horizon has been widened as vehicles attempted to bypass these wrecks and find better going through the snow and mud. The thaw would often reveal the grim sight of crushed bodies which had been hidden by the snow.

ABOVE: A contrast in modes of transport: a horse-drawn *panje* wagon by an abandoned German Ju 52/3m transport aircraft which crash landed near Kiev in 1944 and is now being stripped for spares. The distinctive corrugated aluminium skin of the aircraft which can be seen on the starboard wing earned it the nickname 'Iron Annie'. After the Battle of Stalingrad, the Soviet Air Force repaired more than 80 Ju 52s and the paramilitary airline Aeroflot then used them. Eventually, the Soviet Union would be the second-largest user of the Ju 52 after Germany. Some examples of the aircraft are still flying today.

RIGHT:. The devastation of a German soft-skinned convoy, shot up and looted by Soviet troops on 23 February 1944, in the Korsun-Shevchenkovskiy pocket. The extreme cold of the Eastern Front played havoc with vehicle lubricants and even the elasticity of Buna, the artificial rubber developed for vehicle tyres. In the morning, drivers would start small fires to warm the engines before starting. In retreat, German troops abandoned broken-down vehicles and crowded onto the remaining trucks.

ABOVE: A young sentry of the 2nd Ukrainian Front stands guard over a battle-damaged Junkers Ju 52 transport aircraft. He is talking to a Soviet Air Force pilot and a man who, by his less military appearance, may be a *Politruk* political officer. They have come to visit the wreck near the Korsun-Shevchenkovskiy pocket in the early months of 1944. At the close of the war, with tens of thousands of homes in ruins in the western Soviet Union and not yet repaired or rebuilt, the corrugated fuselages of downed Ju 52s made temporary homes for some Soviet families living near abandoned airfields.

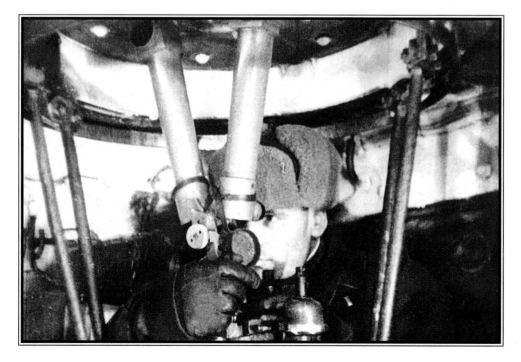

LEFT: Using some 'scissors' binoculars, a Soviet artilleryman calculates the range of a target. The binoculars, widely known as 'donkey's ears', allowed men to observe over the parapet of a trench or through a hatch unhindered by the enemy – although the lenses could become a target to a sharp-eyed soldier. As the two lenses were further apart than a pair of human eyes, they were able to determine ranges much more successfully. Both sides used similar types of binoculars throughout the war.

ABOVE: Russian soldiers and civilians gather around a downed aircraft shrouded in white camouflage. Its shape suggests that it may be a USAAF 8th Air Force B-17 Fortress flown in shuttle missions from Britain to attack targets in eastern Germany and land in the Soviet Union. On 21/22 June 1944, 114 bombers undertaking this type of operation had landed at Poltava in the Ukraine. They were tracked by the Luftwaffe and, in a daring night raid, long-range bombers of the IV Air Corps destroyed 43 B-17 bombers and 15 P-51 Mustang fighters.

BELOW:. Soviet infantry of the 1st Ukrainian Front dressed in *shapka-ushanka* (fur cap with flaps), *polushubok* (short sheepskin coats) and *valenki* (felt boots) hitch a ride on a white camouflaged T-34 as they drive through the outskirts of the town of Brody in the Lvov region in the early spring of 1944. Although some men are huddled on the turret, the best position on the tank is on the rear deck, out of the wind and with the warm air from the engine rising through the louvres – the slatted hatches that give access to the engine.

LEFT: A cluster of German box-bodied trucks which may have been a head-quarters or signals formation abandoned in the winter wastelands of the Korsun-Shevchenkovskiy pocket, seen from an aircraft in the Ukraine in 1944. The photograph shows the flat and featureless nature of the fields of the Soviet collective farms, with the horizon visible in the far distance. It was terrain like this that began to pall on German soldiers who may well have grown up in industrial cities and small rural communities. To them, the country seemed simply too big to conquer.

BELOW: Wheels churn in the snow, as Soviet soldiers of the 1st Ukrainian Front clad in *polushubok* (short sheepskin coats) push a US-supplied ton 4 x 4 Weapons Carrier through drifts on the outskirts of Ternopol in the Ukraine, in March 1944. The absence of good roads in the East and the autumn rains, snow and the consequent mud could immobilise even the best-designed vehicles. Nicknamed 'General Winter' by the Allies, these extremes were a significant contribution to the German defeat.

ABOVE: Hugging the buildings for cover, a patrol of the 1st Czechoslovakian Army Corps works it way through a Ukrainian village, in the early months of 1944. The men wear the long white camouflaged cloaks first introduced in the war with Finland in 1939–40. They would later be replaced with more practical two-piece garments. The soldier in the foreground is armed with the five-round 7.62mm (0.3in) Mosin Nagant M1891/30 bolt-action rifle. The cruciform folding spike bayonet has been swung forwards and locked against the barrel. The relatively old equipment and clothing issued to these soldiers may reflect the Soviet high command's attitude to men whose country had, since the late 1930s, been regarded as a satellite and even an ally of Nazi Germany. Czechoslovakia had been split up by the Nazis and its considerable industrial might harnessed for war production.

RIGHT: The understrength crew of this Soviet 76.2mm (3.0in) Field Gun Model 1939 (76-39) in Kerch in the Crimea, in April 1944, has received orders to engage a new target and is now struggling to move its alignment to the right – hard work with a 1570kg (3461lb) gun in soft ground in April 1944. The 6.4kg (14.1lb) shells seen in the foreground are stacked ready for the next fire mission. The gun had a maximum range of 13,290m (14,534yds) and, like most Soviet guns of this generation, an anti-tank capability with solid shot.

CHAPTER NINE

Red Summer

Crushing the Fascists

O n 8 April 1944, the Soviet offensive by the 4th Ukrainian Front under Tolbukin and the Coastal Army under Yeremenko in the Crimea opened against the German 17th Army in the Crimea. The Soviet bombardment of Sevastopol was twice as heavy as that employed by the Germans in their attack in 1942. On 12 May, against Hitler's orders, the garrison of 12 German and Romanian divisions surrendered, yielding 25,000 prisoners.

LEFT: The shattered remains of a Luftwaffe Heinkel He III bomber – the destruction to fuselage suggests that the 3250kg (7165lb) bomb load has been hit by AA fire. The He III was an enormously versatile aircraft.

FAR LEFT: Armourers from the Soviet Naval Air Force in the Black Sea Fleet load bombs onto a Beriev MBR-2bis short-range maritime reconnaissance flying boat in the Baltic.

THE DEATH OF ARMY GROUP CENTRE

On 22 June 1944, the Red Army opened Operation Bagration against Army Group Centre. Army Group Centre's commander, Field Marshal Ernst Busch, had requested permission to withdraw to stronger positions, but his request had been refused by Hitler. In huge armoured thrusts, the Soviet armoured forces encircled and cut off German forces in the Vitebsk, Mogilev and Bobruysk areas. In four weeks, they advanced 724km (450 miles) and, by 13 July, had reached the Polish border. Behind them were 158,000 dead or captured German troops, 2000 armoured vehicles and 57,000 motor vehicles. The success of Operation Bagration was, if anything, even greater than the Wehrmacht's triumphs of the summer of 1941, as the offensive was conducted against prepared and experienced German troops rather than frightened Russian conscripts. The Germans were hampered in their efforts at defence by a widescale partisan uprising which was timed to coincide with the offensive.

On 20 July 1944, a time bomb exploded under a table during a conference at Hitler's headquarters, the *Wolfsschanze* (Wolf's Lair) at Rastenburg in East Prussia. It had been placed by Lieutenant-Colonel Claus Graf von Stauffenberg in an attempt by a group of Christians and liberals to rid Germany of Hitler and end a hopeless, destructive war. Hitler (and his staff) survived the attack and most of the conspirators were tracked down and killed. Field Marshal Rommel was given the chance to commit suicide. The Führer now became ever more irrational, but was also convinced that his survival had been divinely ordained.

THE WARSAW RISING

On 1 August, with Soviet forces advancing, the Polish Home Army under General Tadeusz Bor-Komorovski rose to liberate the national capital, Warsaw, before the Russians arrived. On Stalin's orders, when the Soviet forces of the 1st and 2nd Belorussian Fronts reached the River Vistula, they halted. The operational explanation was the need to regroup for the final assault into the Reich. What is also certain is that Stalin wanted any potential non-Communist leadership to be destroyed and so he left Warsaw to fight for its life, despite their pleas for assistance. The battle lasted until 2 October, by which time most of the city was in ruins. It was finally 'liberated' by the Russians on 17 January 1945.

ABOVE: The crews of two Soviet M1942 ZIS-3 76mm (2.99in) guns of the 3rd Ukrainian Front follow the pieces into Odessa following its liberation in April 1944. The 76mm anti-tank gun weighed 1150kg (2535lbs) in action and used a modified version of the 57mm (2.24in) gun carriage. To the left of the crews, a US-supplied $\frac{1}{2}$ ton 4 x 4 Weapons Carrier drives past. This versatile vehicle, introduced in 1942, was produced by Dodge, Ford and International, and known by US soldiers as the 'Beep'.

LEFT: This triple 7.62mm (0.3in) Pulemet Maksima Obrazets 1910 Maxim AA machine-gun crew has dispensed with the water cooling jacket around the barrels in favour of a perforated sleeve similar to the US .30 Browning. In winter, the water cooling jacket would possibly present the problem of freezing and an air-cooled barrel would be lighter and easier to elevate and traverse. Later water-cooled marks of the Maxim had a large tractor-filler cap on top of the jacket that allowed the gunner to cram in snow if necessary.

LEFT: An ISU152 from a troop commanded by Lieutenant Mitzkevich, part of the 60th Army part of the 1st Ukrainian Front, grinds past ruined buildings in Pernopol on 15 April 1944. The ISU152 was a formidable combat vehicle. Weighing about 46,000kg (101,412lbs), it had armour that ranged from 30mm (1.18in) to 90mm (3.54in), but its main asset was the 152mm (5.98in) gun howitzer. This weapon fired a 48.8kg (107.6lb) armour-piercing high-explosive shell that could penetrate 124mm (4.88in) of armour at 1000m (1094yds).

ABOVE: A Soviet soldier from a company commanded by Captain Sharygin fires a burst from his PPSh-41 submachine gun, as a squad storms down a railway cutting towards the station at Karpaty, in the western Ukraine, on 29April 29 1944. The man receiving first aid for his head wound looks rather contrived – he would not have thanked a medical orderly for making him such an obvious target with such a conspicuously white bandage. Soviet frontline first aid was rudimentary compared to that of the Germans and particularly to that of the well-resourced Western Allies.

RIGHT: Dressed in *vatnaya telogreika* (padded jackets), a Soviet assault squad storms a German position in a heavy engineering plant in Kerch, in April, 1944. Factories and major public buildings made ideal defensive positions, as they were normally well built from stone or concrete, and often reinforced with steel beams. Cellars and sewers in cities provided cover and access to other districts for reinforcements and ammunition resupply, as well as bombproof headquarters and dressing stations.

THE AIR BATTLE

The Red Air Force had suffered badly in 1941–42, but, by the time of the battle of Stalingrad, it had new, fast, well-armed aircraft and flying aces of both sexes.

BELOW: In 1944, the combat ace F. I. Shikunov, a fighter pilot with the Soviet Air Force, stands by his US-supplied Bell P-63A Kingcobra, with its 'kills' marked along the fuselage. Two-thirds of all the total Kingcobra production of 3305 went to the Soviet Union. The aircraft was used largely for ground-attack operations, with its armament including a 37mm (1.46in) cannon.

RIGHT: A Tupolev SB-2bis bomber is wheeled out from its wooded dispersal area. The Tupolev SB-2bis had a crew of three and was powered by two 830 hp M-100 engines that gave a maximum speed of 410km/h (255mph). The bomber carried a maximum bomb load of 1000kg (2205lbs). These aircraft were first used in the Spanish Civil War, but were obsolescent by 1941 and were used principally in night attacks against German troop concentrations before later being relegated to training roles.

RIGHT: A ZIS-5 fuel tanker pumps aviation fuel into a Lavochkin La-5FN fighter of the Soviet Air Force. The fighter made its operational debut at Stalingrad in late 1942 and proved more than a match for the Luftwaffe Bf 109 fighters. By the end of the war, over 10,000 had been built. The La-5 was armed with two 20mm (0.79in) ShVAK or 23mm (0.91in) NS cannon in the upper cowling and could carry 300kg (661lbs) of bombs underwing. It had a top speed of 648km/h (403mph) and normal range of 765km (475 miles).

BELOW: As the sun sets in 1944, a Soviet Air Force Ilysuhin DB-3F bomber squadron of the 1st Ukrainian Front receives a last-minute morale-boosting talk. Briefings for the mission from the squadron leader and intelligence officer would have taken place indoors with maps indicating targets, navigation features, weather conditions and likely enemy Flak and fighter defences. Here, the squadron's political officer – *politicheskii rukovoditel (Politruk)* or *Kommissar* (Commissar) – may be speaking to the air crew, exhorting them to fulfil their mission against the 'Fascists'.

LEFT: These US-supplied 6 x 4 Studebaker 2$\frac{1}{2}$-ton trucks, having just been moved across the River Dniepr in 1944, are fitted with M13 16-rail launchers and are being prepared for the 132mm (5.20in) *Katyusha* rockets. The rockets are stacked to the rear of the vehicle. The rails for the M13 launcher were 4877m (5334yds) long and could be elevated to 45 degrees and traversed 10 or 20 degrees, according to the chassis. The sight used with the launcher was the standard Soviet MP41 dial sight used for mortars.

RIGHT: Soviet truck-mounted M13 16-rail launchers at maximum elevation loaded with 132mm (5.20in) *Katyusha* rockets close to the River Dniepr in 1944. The rockets, which had a 18.5kg (40.8lb) warhead, were developed from research that began in 1933. Travelling at 355m/s (358yds/sec), they had a maximum range of 8500m (9296yds). The 7.08kg (15.6lb) propellant was probably solventless cordite, but there are also references to Soviet munitions factories using black powder as the motor propellant. The rockets had the major advantage of being easy to produce, and their lack of accuracy meant that poor machining was not a problem. Firing a salvo of 16 rockets also had a significant psychological effect, as the Germans themselves well knew: they developed various rocket systems (such as the *Nebelwerfer*) which were used on all the fronts during the war.

RIGHT: Near Sapun Mountain in the Crimea, a battery of dug-in Soviet 203mm (7.99in) M1931 howitzers prepares to fire in May 1944. The sight settings are being checked. The tracked carriage may have been developed by the huge Soviet tractor industry. It provided a steady base for firing and spread the 17,700kg (29,022lb) weight of the howitzer over a wider area.

LEFT: Soviet troops of the 2nd Guards Army of the 4th Ukrainian Front race down the side of a deep gully in Perekop, in the Crimea, in May 1944. These dry gullies provided cover on the open steppe and were a route from the banks of the Volga into Stalingrad during the fighting in 1942–43. In summer, both sides used them as holding areas for prisoners, as covered start lines for an assault where troops could wait safely, as casualty clearing stations and for dug-in headquarters.

RIGHT: A German 88mm (3.46in) Pak anti-tank gun pit on the Khersones headland in the Crimea is pulverised by Soviet artillery fire on 12 May 1944. Wicker ammunition containers are scattered around the position and the body of one of the crew lies in the entrance of one of the ammunition bunkers. Although the German Army became expert builders of field defences, as well as permanent concrete positions, the enormous weight of Soviet artillery fire would either destroy the position or stun or kill the soldiers.

RIGHT: A German 75mm (2.95in) Sturmgeschütz 40 Ausf G or Stug III assault gun abandoned near the coast at Khersones, in the Crimea, during the assault on Sevastopol by the 4th Ukrainian Front and the Coastal Army in May 1944. After a massive bombardment, the German 17th Army was forced to surrender, and no less than 12 German and Romanian divisions were eliminated and 25,000 prisoners taken, despite Hitler's orders to the contrary. The position of this assault gun suggests that it may have been covering the final amphibious withdrawal in which 38,000 soldiers escaped to the Black Sea port of Constanta in Romania.

LEFT: A light anti-aircraft position aboard the warship *Soobrazitelniy.* Although the rating and his observer with scissors binoculars look suitably businesslike for the photograph, the DShK 1938 12.7mm (0.5in) heavy machine gun appears to be unloaded. The gun is air cooled and, in order to speed up this process by increasing its surface area, it has concentric ridges around the barrel. The distinctive flash eliminator at the muzzle reduces the flame when the gun is fired and directs it sideways.

RIGHT: A torpedo is swung aboard a Soviet warship in the Black Sea Fleet. The six cruisers and 21 destroyers had deck-mounted triple torpedo tubes; however, the fleet also had 84 motor torpedo boats, as well as 47 submarines at the beginning of the war. As a result, the magazines in the naval base at Sevastopol had held a huge stock of torpedoes, as well as ammunition for guns of all calibres, much of which was lost when the port had fallen in 1942. Until Sevastapol's recapture, the fleet had taken refuge in ports near the Turksh coast.

ABOVE: A park of German guns and artillery equipment captured in Odessa in April 1944. In the foreground are two gun limbers for 105mm (4.13in) leFH howitzers, while in the background is a 50mm (1.97in) Pak 38.L/60 anti-tank gun and beyond it a 150mm (5.90in) sFH 18 howitzer. Although half-track prime movers were used to tow heavy artillery, calibres such as the 105mm leFH were often towed by teams of horses hitched to the limber that in turn towed the gun.

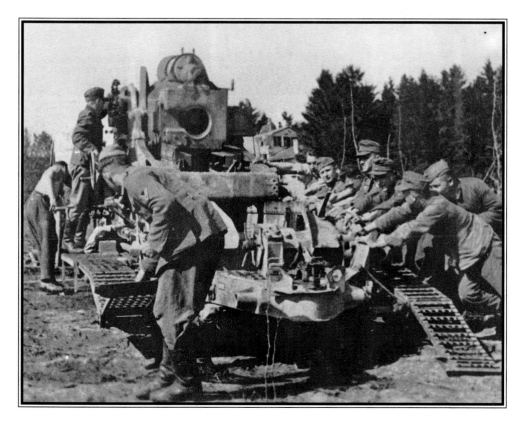

LEFT: German gunners swing a 210mm (8.27in) Mörser 18 on its turntable base in June 1944. The turntable allowed the gun to fire a 133kg (293lb) shell up to 16,700m (18,263yds) with great accuracy. The gun weighed 16,700kg (36,817lbs) in action, so moving it required considerable muscle power. The *Obergefreiter* (Senior Corporal) on the left is folding back one of the hinged walkways mounted on the carriage so that it does not stick on the ground as the gun traverses in a clockwise direction. A gunner on the walkway checks the gun's alignment to the target.

ABOVE: Soviet soldiers stroll past the corpses of three soldiers of the 1st Battalion of Fusilier Regiment 27, killed in hand-to-hand fighting in Mogilev in Belorussia. The city was liberated in June 1944 by Major General I. D. Chernyakhovsky's 2nd Belorussian Front. The city defended by 39th Corps, part of the German 4th Army, was overwhelmed by a massive Soviet summer offensive called Operation Bagration. Army Group Centre lost no less than 30 divisions in the course of the operation, and this was arguably the German Army's greatest defeat in World War II – even greater than their loss at Stalingrad.

RIGHT: Soviet troops slog past abandoned German *Panzerfaust* one-shot anti-tank weapons in the town of Berestechko, in the Volin Region, in July 1944. These are the early marks of the weapon that had only a 30m (33yd) range, but a hollow-charge warhead which could penetrate 140mm (5.51in) and 200mm (7.87in) of armour. The short range made them unpopular with German soldiers, as they had to remain still and undetected until the tank was virtually on top of them, but, by the end of the war, the range of the *Panzerfaust* had been increased to a less dangerous (for the user) 100m (109yds).

RIGHT: Soviet artillerymen load 132mm (5.20in) *Katyusha* (Little Katy) rockets on M13 16-rail launchers mounted on US-supplied 6 x 4 Studebaker 2¹/₂-ton trucks in June 1944 during Operation Bagration. Two men are needed to carry the weight of the 42.5kg (93.7lb) rocket safely. Being fin-stabilised, the *Katyusha* rocket was not as complex as German projectiles which had a ring of venturi (narrow exhaust holes) angled to give the rocket a spin in flight. The *Katyusha* continued in use after the war and was even used by the Viet Minh at the famous siege of Dien Bien Phu in French Indochina in 1954.

BELOW: Smoke rises from a large explosion as Soviet infantry race towards a German position in 1944. If not dead or wounded, the defenders would have been stunned by the blast and, for the assaulting infantry, it would be vital for them to reach the position before the Germans recovered sufficiently to begin active resistance. As they gained experience of Soviet offensive tactics, the Germans built their defences in layers called switch lines, so that they could fall back on these lines set in depth as Soviet pressure built up on each line in turn. In this way the Germans hoped to remove the sting of the Soviet attack.

LEFT: A Soviet artillery officer watches as a gunner elevates the barrel of a 203mm (8in) M1931 howitzer. On the right of the howitzer, another crew member checks the sights and calls out the correction required. To the right of the officer, an ammunition cradle is ready on the ground for loading the next huge round. In action in street fighting in Bukovina, in 1944, the howitzer would be a rather blunt but massively effective weapon against immobile targets such as German strong points and defended buildings.

BELOW: Cossacks of Lieutenant General Kirichenko's 17th Cavalry Corps, which became the 4th Guards Cavalry in August 1942, ride in loose formation across the steppe near Lvov in July 1944. Cavalry were ideal troops for patrolling and reconnaissance in the vast spaces of the Ukraine and Belorussia.

Men and horses could be independent of the logistic train that was needed to support an army moving on tracks or wheels. Although vulnerable to modern automatic weapons, they still retained something of their ancient shock effect for ill-equipped rear echelon troops.

ABOVE: An ISU152 assault gun of the 1st Ukrainian Front rides through a cornfield in the Ukraine in the summer of 1944. The crew members, dressed in black overalls, are also recognisable by their padded *tankobyi shlem* helmets. The three other men dressed in dark tunics and wearing *furazhka* (peaked caps) do not appear to be part of the five-man crew. The relaxed manner of everyone in the picture suggests that they may be officers on a familiarisation visit to the armoured formation.

LEFT: A Soviet GAZ-MM 1,5 ton 4 x 2 cargo truck drives past a line of ISU152 assault guns in Lvov, in the Ukraine, in July 1944. The ISU152 used the chassis of the KV-1 heavy tank, but, whereas the KV-1 had only a 76.2mm (3.0in) gun, the Soviet assault gun took the powerful 152mm (5.98in) M1937 gun howitzer, with its distinctive multi-baffle muzzle brake, as its main armament and carried 20 rounds. These campaign-weary vehicles are loaded with spare fuel drums.

ABOVE: A column of British-supplied Matilda II tanks with some typical Soviet modifications – a small tree trunk as an unditching beam tied to the hull and a fuel drum on the rear deck – in the Lvov region of the Ukraine in the summer of 1944. The tank had a slow top speed of 24km/h (15mph) and the tiny 40mm (1.57in) 2-pounder gun must have seemed puny to Soviet tank crews, but the armour ranging from 20mm (0.79in) to 78mm (3.07in) made it proof against many of the smaller calibre German anti-tank guns.

RIGHT: Soviet artillerymen of the 1st Ukrainian Front use an improvised raft to transport a 76.2mm (3.0in) Field Gun Model 02/30 with the shorter L/30 barrel across the River Zapadni, near the village of Dobrotvor in the Ukraine, on 18 July 1944. To the left, the horses of the gun team have been swum across the river. The ability of Soviet forces to improvise or operate with a minimum of logistic support gave them a tactical flexibility which the Germans often lacked in the harsh conditions of Russia, as the Germans would wait for the proper equipment to arrive before crossing.

RIGHT: Standing on a knocked-out German PzKpfw IV Ausf H fitted with *Schürzen* spaced armour, a Soviet Army cameraman films SU85 assault guns as, laden with infantry of the 1st Ukrainian Front, they drive through a Russian village in the Lvov area in July–August 1944. Approaching in the opposite direction along the road is a US-supplied $\frac{1}{2}$ ton 4 x 4 Weapons Carrier. With US-supplied wheeled vehicles and its own excellent tanks, the Soviet Army had become a mobile and powerful force well capable of the *Blitzkrieg* tactics that the Germans had seen as their preserve.

ABOVE: Infantry soldiers of the 1st Ukrainian Front dash forwards supported by an IS2 heavy tank in the summer of 1944 in the Ukraine. The long 122mm (4.80in) M1943 gun with its distinctive overhang was an extremely powerful weapon; however, it fired two-part ammunition. Normally, tanks had one-part 'fixed' ammunition and so only 28 rounds could be carried. The IS2 was used in action for the first time in February 1944, at Korsun Shevcherkov. At the close of the war, the Kirov factory produced the superb IS3, with its distinctive sloped 'frying pan' turret.

ABOVE: A PM1910 medium machine-gun crew and a Pulemet Degtyareva Tankovii (DT) light machine-gun crew of the 2nd Belorussian Front aboard an improvised armoured train during the fighting east of Warsaw. The Polish Home Army had mobilised to liberate the capital on 1 August 1944, but, under Stalin's orders, the Soviet advance was slowed so that the non-Communist Polish forces under General Bor-Komorowski were eventually brutally crushed by the Germans commanded by General Bach-Zelewski. The old city of Warsaw was then razed to the ground.

LEFT: A Red Army observer scans the sky as the gunner on a camouflaged armoured train mans a 12.7mm (0.5in) DShK M1938 heavy machine gun. The gun's full designation was Krasnoi Pulemet Degtyarev Shpagin Obrazets 1938G, as the gas-operated mechanism had been designed by Degtyarev and the feed system by Georgiy Shpagin. The anti-aircraft ring sight has an ingenious plumline weight that keeps it correctly aligned to the gunner's eyes. The excellence of the DShK's design has ensured that it is still in service throughout the world.

ABOVE: Smoke engulfs a German PzKpfw V Panther tank which was part of the 18th Army of Army Group North. It was destroyed by the 136th Guards Heavy Self-propelled and Tank Regiment of Melitopol, part of the 3rd Baltic Front, during fighting in Tartu, Estonia, in September 1944. Despite the experience of their crews and the quality of the vehicles, German tanks were now so outnumbered that they fell easy prey to Soviet tanks and assault guns.

BELOW: Framed by the torpedo tubes of a destroyer from the same flotilla, a Red Navy ship cuts through the Black Sea. The Axis forces never occupied the entire coastline of the Black Sea, so that, although Soviet ships were forced almost down to the Turkish border on the Black Sea coast, they managed to hang on and were able to assist in the counterattack against Sevastopol in 1944.

CHAPTER TEN

Balkan Blitzkrieg

Exit the Axis Allies

Soviet forces entered Romanian territory on 20 August 1944 and, on 25 August, following a popular uprising against the German garrison in Romania, King Michael switched allegiances and declared war on Germany. In fighting against their former allies, the Romanians took 5437 prisoners, including seven generals. Critically, Germany would no longer have access to the Romanian oilfields at Ploesti and its ships, aircraft

LEFT: A Soviet Air Force officer and men examine a captured German Blohm und Voss BV 222 Viking seaplane loaded on a heavy-duty trailer.

FAR LEFT: Soviet soldiers fighting in the ruins of a town. The man in the foreground appears to be armed with a captured 7.92mm (0.31in) German Kar 98K rifle, while the one behind him has the Soviet Army issue Mosin Nagant 7.62mm (0.3in) rifle.

and vehicles would be immobilised through lack of fuel. The Soviet forces now had an additional 14 Romanian divisions fighting for them, forces that would assist in the liberation of Transylvania, Hungary and Slovakia.

On 5 September, Bulgaria, a country that had been within the Axis orbit, but which had played no part in Barbarossa, was invaded by Soviet forces. The operation, which was assisted by local resistance groups, lasted 24 hours. Bulgarian troops then joined Soviet troops fighting in Yugoslavia, having declared war on Germany on 7 September. The Yugoslav capital of Belgrade was liberated by Yugoslav and Russian troops on 20 October 1944.

The Soviet forces under Marshal Malinovsky launched a two-pronged attack on Hungary. They broke through via Arad on 22 September and linked up with Marshal Petrov's 4th Ukrainian Front. Bad weather and tough German resistance held up the Soviet forces; however, the 3rd Ukrainian Front under Marshal Tolbunkhin reached Lake Balaton and, on Christmas Eve, Soviet forces encircled the Hungarian capital of Budapest.

The garrison, survivors of Army Group South commanded by General Friessener, fought desperately in the sewers and ruins of the city. By the beginning of February, they were

surviving on a ration of 75g (3oz) of bread a day. On the night of 11/12 February, some 16,000 of the garrison attempted to break out, but only a few hundred reached safety. On 13 February, the surviving 33,000 defenders surrendered.

In March, in a final attempt to secure the Hungarian oilfields, the German 6th Army and 6th Panzer Army were ordered by Hitler to counterattack the Soviet armies. The 3rd Ukrainian Front counterattacked and rolled on. On 20 March, Soviet forces were at the Austrian border.

VIENNA TAKEN

On 13 April, Vienna was captured by Malinovsky's and Tolbunkhin's forces after considerable street fighting. In the final battle, the 88mm (3.46in) guns of the 6th Battery, Flak Reserve Regiment 61 at Vienna-Kagran, crewed by teenage girls from the *Bund Deutscher Mädel* (BdM), the German Girls' League, went into action in the anti-tank role against advancing Soviet armour.

Three days later, at 0500 hours, the 1st Belorussian Front under Zhukov began the assault on Berlin. An hour and half later, the 1st Ukrainian Front under Konev swung north to join in the destruction of the capital of the Thousand Year Third Reich.

LEFT: Soviet artillery crews sit casually on their US Studebaker 6 x 4 2½-ton trucks, fitted with M13 16-rail launchers for 132mm (5.20in) *Katyusha* (Little Katy) rockets. The fin-stabilised rockets were developed under great secrecy before the war by an Army engineer named Petropavlovsky and the final work was completed by Andre Kostikov. The rockets perhaps could have been called 'Kostikov's Guns', but the name *Katyusha* stuck – the Germans knew them as 'Stalin Organs' because of the distinctive shriek from the motors. The first rockets went into action on 15 July 1941, less than two months after the German invasion.

LEFT: In preparation for a mission, Soviet paratroops board fast patrol boats of the Dnepropetrovsk River Fleet. Powered by an aircraft engine, armoured and fitted with a T-34 tank turret in the bow, these fast craft with a low silhouette operated with greater autonomy than conventional warships and were rather more effective than the capital ships of the Baltic and Black Sea fleets as they were less easy for the Germans to intercept. Many rivers in Russia and the Ukraine, such as the Volga and the Don, were wide enough for larger torpedo boats to navigate.

RIGHT: Armoured fighting vehicles (AFVs) loaded on railway flat cars and covered with tarpaulins wait in a siding. The tarpaulins are not to protect the AFVs from the elements, but to conceal them from aerial reconnaissance or observers on the ground. Identifying vehicles would enable intelligence officers to establish the type of unit that was being transported and whether the AFVs had been upgraded. The Soviet Army continued this practice of concealment into the 1980s.

RIGHT: Holder of the Order of the Great Patriotic War and the Order of the Red Star, Major M. A. Bezdkevich, stands by his Polikarpov U-2VS (Po-2) close-support light bomber. The two- or three-seater biplane had one 7.62mm (0.3in) ShKAS machine gun and a 250kg (551lb) bomb load. The maximum speed of 150km/h (93mph) meant that the Po-2s normally launched their attacks at night, as they would be extremely vulnerable during the day. The propeller-driven aircraft, which first flew in 1928, was still being built in the 1950s. A number of captured aircraft equipped a Luftwaffe *Staffel* composed of ex–Soviet Air Force volunteers in 1942–43. The Soviets were keen exponents of night raids on front line forces, and virtually anything that could fly was used to disturb the Germans.

BELOW: With air superiority ensured by low-flying Soviet Air Force fighters, T-34 tanks move in open formation across the grasslands of the Ukraine. From 1943 onwards, the German forces in the Soviet Union were on the receiving end of the lessons in deep penetration armour tactics which they had demonstrated in western Europe and Russia. The young Soviet generals and marshals had been adept pupils, and the thrusts by their armies and fronts cut off huge pockets of German troops who had been forbidden to retreat by their Führer. Although Hitler may have been motivated by a desire to keep his oil-supplying Balkan allies in the Axis with a show of holding the conquests made in 1941 and 1942, his intransigence cost the German Army thousands of precious troops.

ABOVE: Smoke pours from a knocked-out German PzKpfw IV tank. The tracks and side armour are protected by *schürzen* (skirts). In action, these plates were often torn off. The turret has spaced armour attached to a steel frame. The stowage bin on the rear of the turret and crew hatches are open. The open stowage bin suggests that Soviet soldiers may have had a good search of the vehicle for loot before it was set on fire for the benefit of the photographer.

LEFT: Protected from the elements by his *plasch-nakidka* (rain cape), a Soviet soldier of the 1st Ukrainian Front stands guard with his PPSh-41 submachine gun in the ruins of a town in the Vinnytsya of the Ukraine in 1944. The cape had a hood large enough to cover a helmet and could be used as part of a four-man tent. Although their robust and simple weapons were excellent, Soviet soldiers were keen to acquire items of German personal equipment such as binoculars, while German mess tins and eating utensils made living in the field more bearable.

LEFT: Plodding at the rear of a column of soldiers, two Soviet machine gunners carry the wheeled base for two Sokolov mounts for Maxim 1910 water-cooled machine guns in Karpaty in the autumn of 1944. In front of them are soldiers armed with the 7.62mm (0.3in) Mosin Nagant M1891/30 bolt-action rifle. With the shield, the machine-gun mount weighed a hefty 45.2kg (99.6lbs) and gave the weapon a degree of mobility; however, it could only effectively be towed across flat, stable ground.

RIGHT: A comprehensively destroyed German *Nashorn* (Rhinoceros) or *Hornisse* (Hornet) SdKfz 164 self-propelled 88mm (3.46in) Pak 43/1/71 anti-tank gun at Drogobich in August 1944. Some 473 vehicles were built by the Deutsche Eisenwerke Teplitz-Schoenau works using the PzKpfw IV bogie units and the PzKpfw III final drive assemblies. The vehicle weighed 2.5 tons and entered service in November 1942. It had a crew of five who were protected from the front and sides, but not from above.

LEFT: Two Soviet Air Force fighter pilots, both holders of the Hero of the Soviet Union, stand by the wreckage of a Luftwaffe Ju 52 'Iron Annie' trimotor transport aircraft. Ju 52 had a crew of two or three, and could carry 12 parachutists or 17 men, although in emergencies they were often overloaded. The Ju 52 was powered by three 830hp BMW engines and had a top speed of 265km/h (165mph). Its ceiling was 5500m (18,045ft) and range of 1287km (800 miles). About 3000 aircraft were produced between 1939 and 1945.

RIGHT: Soviet anti-tank gunners of the 1st Ukrainian Front deploy two 45mm (1.77in) Model 1942 guns in Poland in the autumn of 1944. The exposed position that they have adopted suggests that this is a drill – perhaps each crew is competing to see who can be fastest into action. The Model 1942 gun was an updated version of the Model 1932.

LEFT: In the cramped interior of a turret, Soviet sailors prepare to load a M1939 KS-12 85mm (3.35in) anti-aircraft gun. The gun crew members wear steel helmets more as protection against the sharp angles inside the turret than against shell fragments and shrapnel. High-explosive shells weighed 9.5kg (20.9lbs) and, as long as there was a reliable ammunition supply, the seven-man crew could fire between 15 and 20 rounds a minute.

BELOW: Smoke and dust shroud a battery of 152mm (5.98in) howitzers as they deliver a concentrated barrage on German positions in the Ukraine in the summer of 1944. The big guns could fire a 40kg (88lb) high-explosive shell or a 51kg (112lb) semi–armour-piercing shell with a muzzle velocity of 432m/s (472yds/sec). The crew of seven could fire between three and four rounds a minute.

RIGHT: Massive firepower on the move: a column of Soviet ISU152 heavy assault guns of the 1st Ukrainian Front moves through the Chenstokhov region of Poland in January 1945. Infantry ride on the vehicle to provide it with local defence, as it had only one machine gun – a 12.7mm (0.5in) anti-aircraft gun mounted in an exposed position on the roof. Tanks normally had a co-axial machine gun in the turret, one in the hull glacis plate and sometimes an anti-aircraft machine gun on the turret roof. Without machine guns armour could not suppress enemy infantry, and that infantry could be carrying an anti-tank *Panzerfaust* or magnetic mine.

RIGHT: A Soviet 7.62mm (0.3in) DP light machine-gun crew takes aim at a distant target. The picture is obviously posed as the crew of an automatic weapon would never take up an exposed position in a window where the muzzle flash and dust would be obvious to the enemy. Crews would normally site the weapon well back from the window inside the room. Even though this would provide a narrower field of fire, it would also mean that the muzzle flash would not be seen from outside the building by the enemy.

LEFT: Soviet infantry of the 1st Ukrainian Front in Poland. They are dressed in *shinel* (greatcoats) and *shapka-ushanka* (fur caps with ear flaps), and are standing on the warm rear decks of ISU152 heavy assault guns, where the heat rises from the 600hp engine in the winter cold of January 1945. The ISU152 weighed approximately 46,000kg (101,412lbs) and had armour ranging from 30mm (1.18in) to 90mm (3.54in). The ISU152K, with external stowage and engine improvements, remained in production until 1952.

CHAPTER ELEVEN

Advance to the Oder

Breaking into the Third Reich

In January 1945, the Red Army held a line along the border of East Prussia down the Narew River to Warsaw and then roughly along the Vistula River. After the defeat of Army Group Centre, it held a clear military superiority over the German forces. There were more than six million Soviet troops and over 91,000 tanks against just over three million Germans with 28,5000 tanks.

LEFT: Soviet gunners await the order to fire their 122mm (4.80in) M1938 howitzers at positions held by remnants of Army Group Centre in East Prussia in January 1945. The pockets on the coast held out until 9 May 1945.

FAR LEFT: A Soviet officer checks the inventory of a small arms and *Panzerfaust* anti-tank ammunition abandoned by the German Army in a wood in 1945.

BIG GUNS

In 1945, the Red Army was equipped with some excellent weapons, including the superior IS-2 tank with its 122mm (4.80in) gun, as well the T-34 M1944 with an 85mm (3.35in) gun. Although the German forces had the Tiger II and excellent Panther tanks, they were very short of fuel. The quality of the German soldiers was varied and included men of the *Volkssturm* (People's Army, literally the 'Peoples' Storm'). The *Volkssturm* was the German civilian home defence force established in September 1944 and included all civilian males between the ages of 16 and 60 who were capable of bearing arms.

The Soviet offensive began on 12 January 1945 with a tremendous barrage. It was one week ahead of the date scheduled and was launched to take pressure off the Allies in the Battle of the Bulge. In four days, the attack had ripped a hole 360km (224 miles) wide and 50–160km (31–99 miles) deep and developed into two dozen parallel axes. The two most powerful out of the Vistula bridgeheads were Konev's 1st Ukrainian and Zhukov's 1st Belorussian Fronts, who enjoyed a ten-to-one superiority over the German forces opposing them.

By the end of January, they had reached the original 1939 German–Polish border on the Oder. In early February, Soviet bridgeheads had been established on the west bank of the Oder at Küstrin and Frankfurt. Desperate German counter-attacks at the Stargard railway in mid-February stalled the westward Red Army drive.

SIEGE OF KÖNIGSBERG

The Baltic port of Königsberg (Kaliningrad) was surrounded by the 3rd Belorussian Front under Marshal Ivan Bagramyan. Under the forceful command of General Lasch, however, the garrison held out until 10 April.

The Red Army swung northwards to clear Pomerania and Silesia, where the grandiosely named Army Group Vistula was under the inept command of the *Reichsführer* Heinrich Himmler. Rokossovsky's 3rd Guards Tank Corps spearheaded the push to the Baltic coast and reached it on 1 March. This cut off the German garrisons and depots at Danzig (Gdansk) and Gotenhaven (Gdynia), while supporting Zhukov's drive which reached the coast at Kölberg. The port held out until 18 March.

Four days later, the 1st Belorussian Front launched a flanking attack on Küstrin which fell on 30 March. In Silesia to the south, Konev's 1st Ukrainian and Petrov's 4th Ukrainian Fronts drove towards Grottkau and Moravska Ostrava. In

Breslau, the chief city of Silesia, the population had been evacuated to Dresden and the city declared a fortress. Defended by 35,000 troops, it held out against Soviet attacks and they were reinforced with paratroops through an improvised airstrip. Breslau finally fell on 8 May 1945.

LEFT: Junior Sergeant N. A. Siderenko, a Pulemet Degtyareva Pekhotnii (DP) light machine gunner, takes aim, while the number two V. S. Melnichenko loads the 47-round drum magazine. This crew, part of the 1st Ukrainian Front, is in position on the River Oder in the winter of 1945. A DP crew carried three drum magazines in a metal box. Designed by Vasily Alexeyevich Degtyarev, an engineer at the Tula arsenal in the 1920s, the gun weighed 11.9kg (26.2lbs) and was a simple gas-operated weapon with only six moving parts which fired at 520 to 580 rounds a minute.

BELOW: A 76.2mm (3.0in) Infantry Gun M1927 detachment of the 1st Ukrainian Front commanded by Guards Sergeant Gudz takes up a position in a town near the River Oder in Germany in January 1945. The little field piece weighed 780kg (1720lbs) in action, but could fire a 6.21kg (13.7lb) shell to 8555m (9356yds), which made it an ideal weapon for street fighting. The big 1143mm (45in) wheels made it easy to manoeuvre and also provided the crew with extra protection. Although the doors of the bar behind are open, it is unlikely that any service would be available.

RIGHT: Soviet infantry run past the gutted shop front of a store in the north German town of Gleiwitz on 1 February 1945. Although the shop has burned out and been completely destroyed, the display cabinet on the left has miraculously survived. Until the very last days of the war, the rubble from bombing in German towns and cities was always cleared away and stacked to one side to leave the roads clear for any military vehicles by conscripted or slave labour which was organised for that very purpose. The damage in this town may therefore have been caused by street fighting. To some of the Russians fighting through the town it would have evoked memories of the fighting at Stalingrad.

LEFT: A 76.2mm (3.0in) Infantry Gun Model 1927 (76-27) crew of the 59th Army of the 1st Ukrainian Front commanded by Senior Sergeant Prokofiev in action in the streets of Gleivitz, a town on the old Polish–German border, in 1945. After 1939, the area that included Gleiwitz was occupied by the Germans and became the General Government administered by the brutal Hans Frank from Wavel castle in Krakow. In 1944, Frank fled in the face of the advance by Soviet forces.

RIGHT: German trenches, apparently abandoned without a fight, dug on open ground outside the town of Guttentag, now Dobrodzen, in 1945. At the close of the war, the Germans often used slave labour or impressed civilians to assist in building defences. These could include trenches, bunkers or anti-tank ditches. Lack of heavy timber has meant that these well-revetted (reinforced) trenches at Guttentag do not have bunkers for machine guns, nor do they have barbed wire obstacles to their front to delay an infantry assault.

LEFT: A battery of 122mm (4.80in) M1939 howitzers of the 3rd Belorussian Front opens fire on Königsberg. The howitzer had a crew of eight and fired 21.8kg (48.1lb) high-explosive shell to a maximum range of 11,800m (12,905yds). The garrison of the Baltic port commanded by General Otto Lasch held out until 9 April 1945, when he finally surrendered. Hitler sentenced Lasch to death in absentia and had his family arrested. According to Soviet estimates, more than 27,000 soldiers were taken prisoner.

BELOW: Smoke and dust swirl as soldiers of the 3rd Belorussian Front dash towards an apartment block in Königsberg during fighting in 1945. The city was ringed by two belts of fortifications and the centre protected by eight strong points. While parts of the German garrison became demoralised and a regiment of the 367th Infantry Division surrendered without orders, the 61st Infantry Division fought on for an extra day following the surrender by General Lasch on 9 April 1945.

RIGHT: The sights are checked on a Soviet 203mm (7.99in) M1931 howitzer of the Soviet 2nd Baltic Front on the Baltic coast in spring 1945. In the Kurland Peninsula, some 26 German divisions from Army Group Centre held out until the end of the war. They were renamed Army Group Kurland and were supported by the *Kriegsmarine*, the German Navy, which evacuated 157,000 wounded and 1.5 million refugees, as well as elements of two panzer and four infantry divisions.

LEFT: The crew of a Soviet 203mm (7.99in) M1931 howitzer of the Soviet 2nd Baltic Front on the Baltic coast – most likely the same crew as that shown above – ready the weapon for action in the spring of 1945. The rammer lies on the trail, while the crew has swung the ammunition hoist round on the left, ready to pick up a 98.5kg (217.2lb) shell. When a big gun such as the M1931 had a full, well-trained crew, steady fire could be kept up despite the relatively crude design of the weapon. Although self-propelled, in reality the gun was so heavy that its manoeuvrability was curtailed, and long distances were travelled by rail.

RIGHT: The crew of a 122mm (4.80in) Howitzer M1938 commanded by Senior Sergeant G. E. Makeev of the 1st Ukrainian Front runs from a shelter to man their gun. Partially camouflaged behind rubble, furniture and a fir tree which also form a barricade, the gun is in a position to cover down the main road, Mendelstrit, in Breslau, Germany, in March 1945. Sergeant Makeev's crew would have been capable of firing five or six rounds a minute and, with a maximum range of 11.8km (7.3 miles), would have no difficulty in engaging targets at the end of a street – even one as long as this. Although the Soviet generals were keen to avoid streetfighting as much as possible for the delay it caused to the advance, it was inevitable.

BELOW: Guards Junior Sergeant V. I. Isakov of the 1st Ukrainian Front engages a target at close range with a 12.7mm (0.5in) Degtyarev Shpagin DShK M1938 heavy machine gun. This gas-operated, air-cooled machine gun fired from a 50-round belt and had an effective range of 1500m (1640yds). For a ground role, the DShK used the Sokolov mount complete with armoured shield. It appears in this case that the shield has been removed to save weight, as the DShK was notoriously heavy, particularly when combined with the Solokov mount. On armoured vehicles, it was fitted with an optical sight for use as an anti-aircraft gun by the vehicle's commander, although it could also be used to suppress infantry.

RIGHT: Red Air Force armourers unload bombs for a squadron of Petlyakov Pe-2 dive-bombers. The Pe-2 could carry 1200kg (2646lbs) of bombs, was powered by two 1100 Klimov M-105R engines and had a top speed of 540km/h (336mph) at 5000m (16,319ft). The crew of three or four included two gunners who operated 7.62mm (0.3in) ShKAS machine guns in dorsal and ventral positions. The Pe-2 was also armed with two nose-mounted 7.62mm machine guns, or one and a 12.7mm (0.5in) machine gun, making it a formidable ground-attack aircraft.

RIGHT: A German 88mm (3.46in) Flak gun abandoned by a shell-blasted box-bodied vehicle in a town in eastern Germany in 1945. As the Soviet forces closed in on Germany, anti-aircraft crews manning 88mm and larger calibre guns were pressed into frontline duty against Soviet tanks. This gun appears to have been used in an anti-aircraft role and then stripped of its wheels, probably to keep another gun or a vehicle on the road in order to allow troops to withdraw. Like petrol and other oil-based products, rubber was in short supply in Germany, and the Germans had to resort to synthetic (and inferior) versions in an attempt to meet demand.

RIGHT: A soldier of the 1st Ukrainian Front commanded by Marshal I. S. Koniev races through woodland in the Brandenberg Forest in Germany in April 1945. He is armed with a Pistolet-Pulemet Sudareva 01943g or PPS43 submachine gun, an all-metal weapon with a folding stock and a box magazine with 35 rounds. The SMG was derived from the PPS42 which had been designed by A. I. Sudarev, an engineer in besieged Leningrad, and used almost no wood in its construction because there was none in Leningrad.

ABOVE: Soldiers of the 1st Ukrainian Front slog towards Berlin in the chill of an April morning in 1945. Unlike the highly mechanised transportation of the Allied armies, the westward advance of the Soviet forces was not by vehicle, but often on horseback, on the back of tanks and assault guns, in captured vehicles and, finally, on foot. These men with their rifles and lack of helmets may be second-line troops sweeping up behind the tanks and their tank descent assault troops.

LEFT: A group of senior Soviet officers, sporting campaign medals and decorations for bravery and professionalism, checks maps and plans prior to the next phase of operations against East Prussia. By 1944–45, Soviet generals had the double advantage of large forces and good equipment. They could afford to use this massed firepower and tanks to punch through the increasingly thinly held German defences and do this at several points along the front, so stretching whatever reserves might be available.

RIGHT: Anti-tank gunners of the 1st Ukrainian Front take up a position covering a street in the town of Kalau in Germany in April 1945. They are manhandling a 57mm (2.24in) Model 43 L/73 gun. This well-designed weapon weighed 1150kg (2535lbs) in action and fired a 3.148kg (6.94lb) shell to a maximum range of 8.4km (5.2 miles). With a muzzle velocity of 1020m/s (1115yds/sec) it could penetrate 140mm (5.5in) of armour at 500m (547yds). An experienced crew could fire 20 rounds a minute.

BELOW: A Soviet 122mm (4.80in) Howitzer M1938 crew commanded by Sergeant Major N. M. Lumanov of the 1st Ukrainian Front prepares it for action near the town of Shtrelen, East Prussia (now Stepelin in Poland) in April 1945. As the barrel is cleaned through, a crew member positions small fir trees around the gun pit as camouflage and a fifth member hammers in pins to secure the split trail carriage. Once in action, the five men would be able to keep up a maximum rate of fire of five to six rounds a minute, engaging targets out to 11.8km (7.3 miles) with 21.8kg (48.0lb) shells.

LEFT: Black exhaust streams from a T-34/85/1 tank of the 1st Ukrainian Front, as it crosses a deserted railway bridge over the Elbe in May 1945. By now the war was almost over, and the tank's commander is sufficiently unworried by the prospect of snipers to sit on the outside of the turret. In the background are the gutted ruins of the city of Dresden in southeastern Germany. In subsequently controversial air raids launched between 13 and 15 February 1945, RAF and USAAF bombers had attacked Dresden, which was filled with refugees from the East. In the deliberately caused intense fire storm that followed the Allied raid, between 30,000 and 60,000 people – mostly civilians – were killed.

LEFT: A US-supplied $^1/_2$ ton 4 x 4 Weapons Carrier tows a canvas-covered M1939 37mm (1.46in) anti-aircraft gun through the streets of Dresden. The gun had a maximum vertical range of 6000m (6562yds) and effective range of 1400m (1531yds); by this stage of the war, the gun crew would have engaged ground targets at ranges of up to 8000m (8749yds). Firing armour-piercing ammunition, it could penetrate 46mm (1.81in) at 500m (547yds). Part of the crew of eight are riding on the gun and the back of the truck.

RIGHT: With the launch rails protected by canvas, which also serves to shelter the crew, US-supplied 6 x 4 Studebaker $2^1/_2$-ton trucks of the 4th Ukrainian Front, fitted with M13 launchers for sixteen 132mm (5.20in) *Katyusha* (Little Katy) rockets, enter the Czech town of Moravia Ostrava in 1945. The alert appearance of the crew belies the fact that the 2nd Ukrainian Front under General Rodion Malinovsky and the 4th under General Ivan Petrov encountered little resistance at the close of the war.

ABOVE: A bullet-scarred tram stands abandoned in the street in the centre of Breslau on 5 May 1945. Although surrounded and under heavy attack by the 6th Army of the 1st Ukrainian Front, the city held out until 7 May. Its Gauleiter Karl Hanke, who had ordered that the Mayor Dr Spielhagen be shot 'for cowardice', fled to the West in a light aircraft before the surrender. It did him no good, however, for he was later captured and shot by Czech partisans.

RIGHT: Two of the four-man crew sit on the outside of a Soviet IS2 tank in an armoured column from the 1st Belorussian Front commanded by Marshal Georgi Zhukov, as it passes an abandoned German truck close to a country estate in Germany in 1945. The IS2's powerful 122mm (4.80in) M1943 gun could penetrate the thick, angled frontal armour of the PzKpfw V Panther, arguably the German's best all-round tank, while its 30mm (1.18in) to 160mm (6.30in) armour made it almost invulnerable to all but the largest calibre anti-tank guns.

CHAPTER TWELVE

Battle for Berlin

Nemesis of the Third Reich

On 12 April 1945 Hitler heard the news of the death of the US President Franklin Roosevelt. Dr Goebbels, the fanatical Nazi Minister of Propaganda, was ecstatic and signalled: 'My Führer, I congratulate you! Roosevelt is dead. It is written in the stars that the second half of April will be the turning point for us.' The Führer was now so far removed from reality that he was consulting astrologers.

THE RED ARMY CLOSES IN

However, the nemesis of the Third Reich was reaching its violent conclusion as the Red Army closed in on Berlin. The Soviet offensive began on 16 April with a huge pincer movement. On the Baltic, the 2nd Belorussian Front under Marshal Rokossovsky pushed across the Oder at Stettin. To his left, the 1st Belarussian Front under Marshal Zhukov had already crossed the River Oder and established a jumping-off point at Küstrin. To the south, the 1st Ukrainian Front under Marshal Konev hooked east and north across the rivers Oder and Neisse. The three fronts had a total of two and a half million troops, 6250 armoured vehicles, 10,400 guns and mortars, and 7500 aircraft.

By 19 April, the Russians had reached the suburbs of Berlin. On 25 April, Zhukov and Konev linked up and Berlin was surrounded. Trapped inside was the garrison of 200,000 and a pocket with about the same number of troops to the west of the city.

Berlin, already badly damaged by RAF raids, would be fought for street by street, from the suburbs to the Reichstag in the centre. The canals, U-Bahn (subway) and vast stone-built buildings with cellars were ideal for street fighting. The

LEFT: Covered by a smoke screen, an SU122 of the 3rd Guards Tank Army of the 1st Ukrainian Front crosses a pontoon bridge over the River Spree, near Cottbus in April 1945.

FAR LEFT: Guards Corporal A. M. Samikin of the 1st Ukrainian Front, armed with a PPS43 submachine gun, advances through a suburban garden in Berlin in April 1945.

outermost belt of the concentric defences was about 32km (20 miles) from the city centre; for the next 16km (10 miles), the S-Bahn served as a defence. Finally, in the centre was the 'Z' (*Zitadelle* – The Citadel), with the government offices and the Führerbunker, the two-storey concrete bunker by the Reich Chancellery where Hitler was now living a troglodyte life. The Citadel was split into eight defence sectors. Sector III to the southeast on the Landwehr canal was defended by men of the *Waffen-SS* Panzer Grenadier Division *Nordland*. This formation contained men who had volunteered for the *Waffen-SS* from Scandinavia, France and, its is believed, even a small group of former British prisoners of war.

HITLER IN THE BUNKER

From his bunker, Hitler continued issuing orders to armies that no longer existed. The last film taken there of Hitler alive shows the Führer walking down a line of *Hitlerjugend* (Hitler Youth 'soldiers') to award them Iron Crosses for their defence of Berlin.

On 20 April, the Führer celebrated his 56th birthday. Among his visitors was the pioneering aviatrix Hanna Reitsch, who evaded Soviet fighters and anti-aircraft fire to land on the Charlottenburger Strasse in the Tiergarten parkland near the bunker. Just a day later, the city became a battleground, with the savage street fighting including heavy artillery fired from point-blank range at German strong points.

On 30 April, Soviet troops of the 171st and 150th Rifle Divisions raced into the ruined Reichstag, climbed to the top and raised the Red Flag of hammer and sickle. On the same day, Hitler shot himself after giving instructions that his body should be burned.

At 1500 hours on 2 May, General Karl Weidling, the Commandant of the Berlin garrison, instructed it to surrender. About 136,000 men marched into captivity. In the fighting between 16 April and 8 May, the Red Army had taken 480,000 prisoners. In the ruins were the bodies of more than 100,000 civilians who had died in the fighting. About 304,000 Soviet soldiers were killed in the battle for Berlin.

In the city, many Red Army soldiers saw murder and rape as their rightful due following the German atrocities committed in Russia. A degree of looting was permitted by the Soviet High Command and soldiers sent home a limited amount of goods. NKVD and GRU officers combed through

German Government archives and public buildings. Some 90 gold bars and more than four and a half million gold coins with a 1945 value of three and a half million dollars were taken from the Reichsbank Berlin in May 1945. Some looting on a larger scale took place on 15 May: a GRU major named Feodor Novokov took gold currency bonds with a 1945 value of 400 million dollars issued against the Westphalia, Weimar Industrial from the Reichsbank.

ABOVE: T-34/85/1 tanks of the 3rd Guards Tank Army of the 1st Ukrainian Front wait in woodland close to Berlin in April 1945. The T-34/85 had a cast steel turret and was armed with an 85mm (3.35in) ZIS-53 gun that had originally been an anti-aircraft gun with 55 rounds. Although the chassis was virtually unchanged from the T-34/76, the increased weight of armour – 60mm (2.36in) in contrast to 45mm (1.77in) – and armament had reduced the top speed to 50km/h (31mph).

BELOW: Tyazholy Tank IS Heavy Tank 'Iosef Stalin' IS2 tanks of the 1st Ukrainian Front camouflaged in a concentration area in woods near Berlin in April 1945. The IS2 was armed with a 122mm (4.80in) M1943 gun with 28 rounds, as well as a 12.7mm (0.5in) anti-aircraft gun and three 7.62mm (0.3in) machine guns. The IS2 was the most powerfully armed tank in World War II and its improved fire control meant that it was more than a match for German Tigers and Panthers.

LEFT: A Soviet T-34/85/1 tank of the 3rd Guards Tank Army commanded by Colonel General V. N. Gordov, part of the 1st Ukrainian Front, grinds into a leafy suburb of Schöneberg in southwest Berlin in April 1945. The Soviet force fought against the remnants of the German 18th Panzer Grenadier Division, as it pushed north and east. It would eventually push through to the western end of the Tiergarten, the park in central Berlin, before fighting came to a halt. Stalin decided to award Zhukov's Belorussian Front the honour of capturing the Reichstag.

RIGHT: A Soviet trucks tows a 100mm (3.94in) Model 1944 anti-tank gun across an improvised bridge over the Spree in Germany in April 1945. The gun weighed 3460kg (7628lbs) in action and had a 5969mm (235in) barrel, yet, despite this size and weight, an experienced crew could fire between eight and ten rounds a minute. The 15.6kg (34.4lb) shell had a muzzle velocity of 900m/s (984yds/sec) and armour penetration of 192mm (7.56in) at 450m (492yds), making it one of the most powerful anti-tank guns produced in World War II. The 1st Ukrainian Front's advance was helped by the fact that Hitler diverted most of his remaining panzer forces to the defence of Prague, convinced the final Soviet offensive would strike there.

LEFT: The battered remains of a small field kitchen near the entrance to a bar in the centre of Berlin bear mute testimony to the way in which the city authorities attempted to keep society functioning normally. Food was distributed to bombed-out families, many of whom had taken up permanent residence in the huge multi-storey concrete Flak towers that doubled as air raid shelters at the western end of the Charlottenburger Chaussee to the west of the German capital.

LEFT: 'Dragon's Teeth' reinforced concrete anti-tank obstacles originally designed by the Germans for their West Wall defences in 1938–39, built to the east of Berlin. The obstacles in this picture are sited to stop tanks moving from left to right, and concealed behind a bank – this would achieve tactical surprise. Tracked vehicles were unable to push through the staggered concrete blocks and, if they did mount them, would end up straddling the blocks or might lose a track.

BELOW: Soviet infantry with a T-34/85 make their way down the tidy suburban streets of outer Berlin in April 1945. The area is away from the major public buildings in the city centre and therefore has not suffered from bombing raids or street fighting. The population, however, would suffer from the looting and rape that Soviet commanders saw as the legitimate spoils of victory for their soldiers and revenge for the German destruction in Belorussia and the Ukraine between 1941 and 1944.

RIGHT: Soldiers of the 1st Ukrainian Front pass the burning stables of a mansion on the outskirts of Berlin on a chill morning in April 1945. Faced with the prospect of occupation by the Soviets, many German families in the east fled after hiding their wealth and sometimes setting fire to their homes. Others, appalled by defeat, chose suicide. After the reunification of Germany in 1989, there were cases of this hidden treasure being recovered by survivors from sites in the former German Democratic Rebublic.

RIGHT: Infantry crowds aboard a T-34 tank of the 3rd Guards Tank Army of the 1st Ukrainian Front, as it grinds past a rococo church on the outskirts of Berlin in April 1945. The relaxed attitude of the soldiers suggests that this an approach march in which, for lack of troop-carrying vehicles, the 3rd Guards Tank Army has simply used its armour to carry infantry to the front line. Only the Germans and Allies afforded their infantry the luxury of trucks for transport.

BELOW: Tanks of the 25th Tank Corps commanded by Major General E. I. Fominich, part of the 3rd Guards Tank Army of the 1st Ukrainian Front, moving through the pine forests on the southwest outskirts of Berlin in April 1945. The 3rd Guards Tank Army would drive deep into the city, reaching its final report line of the fashionable Kurfurstendamm, Berlin's quality shopping street (the equivalent of London's Bond Street), by the time the fighting had ended.

RIGHT: I. A. Morgoon, a soldier of the 1st Ukrainian Front commanded by Marshal Konev, prepares to hand a 3.148kg (6.94lb) shell forwards to Junior Sergeant N. V. Kopilov as he sights a 57mm (2.24in) M1943 L/73 anti-tank gun and prepares to fire a third round on the outskirts of Berlin in April 1945. The gun has been sited in a cramped position on a pavement and so the legs of the split trail, which were taken from the Model 42/SiS 3 76mm (2.99in) field gun, have not been fully spread. The gunners have therefore put wooden logs under the rear of the pneumatic wheels to help absorb more of the recoil force. If they didn't do this, the gun would move after every firing, and they would have to aim it all over again.

RIGHT: A 132mm (5.20in) *Katyusha* (Little Katy) rocket battery waits with rockets loaded in the streets of Berlin as they receive the order of the day, read by the *Politruk* (political officer) or *Kommissar* (Commissar) in April 1945. The battery commander stands to the left, ready to give the order for fire to commence. Although the pressure was on to capture Berlin, clearly there was still time available to stage manage symbolic moments in the final defeat of the Nazi capital.

LEFT: A car from a *Melkerei* (dairy) with its engine stripped out stands in Elizabetstrasse (Elizabeth Street) in Berlin as an apartment block burns in the background. Elizabetstrasse was in Wilmersdorf, the elegant suburbs in the south not far from the central park of the Tiergarten. The Soviet 8th Guards Army and 1st Guards Tank Army pushed aside local counterattacks by the last few tanks of the XVIII Panzer Division and tightened the noose on the centre of Berlin in the last days of April 1945.

LEFT: Soviet T-34/85 tanks rumble through the gutted streets of Berlin. The commanders are sitting looking out of the turret hatches, suggesting that the fighting is over in this area; however, nervous and curious civilians have not yet appeared on the streets, which suggests that it is not long over. Gutted apartment blocks show how devastating RAF and USAAF raids were on the city during the Battle for Berlin. In a single raid on 3 February 1945, 1000 USAAF bombers killed an estimated 25,000 Berliners.

BELOW: A spectacular picture of a 132mm (5.20in) *Katyusha* (Little Katy) M13 16-rail rocket launcher as the 42.5kg (93.7lb) rockets streak away. This Guards rocket regiment commanded by Guards Colonel T. I. Shankin was photographed on an April night in 1945. Rocket artillery has one major drawback, in modern parlance it has a distinctive 'signature' – the flame and smoke and dust kicked up by the motors show clearly where the rockets have been launched.

LEFT: Refugees emerge from the cellars of gutted buildings and pass IS2 tanks of the 1st Belorussian Front in the rubble-clogged streets of Berlin in April 1945. The Soviet tanks have a white band painted around their turrets as an air identification marking to prevent RAF and USAAF fighter bombers attacking them in error. As the Allies and Soviet forces closed in on Germany, there were encounters in the air and finally on the ground.

ABOVE: Buildings along the elegant Elizabetstrasse in Wilmersdorf burn following the final street battles. In the foreground, the street has been dug up either for trenches or a rudimentary anti-tank obstacle. Movement on foot across the exposed ground of a large city street could be lethal during fighting and so sewers were used or crawl trenches were dug to allow infantry to travel more safely between buildings.

RIGHT: Soviet 152mm (5.98in) M1937 gun howitzers, part of the detachment commanded by Guards Lieutenant Grigorov in Berlin in April 1945. The guns are sited on the pavement, which has buckled under their 7117kg (15.823lb) weight, and aligned along the road close to buildings which give them protection and a wider traverse to the left. White flags hang from the apartment windows in the street to spare destruction.

RIGHT: The prototype 88mm (3.46in) Pak 43/3 auf Panzerjäger 38(t) stands battered and abandoned in a street in central Berlin. Developed in late 1944, this vehicle was intended to be part of a new series of powerful tank hunters – *Panzerjäger*. It was based on the Czech 38(t) tank, but had the engine at the front with a Pak 43 mounted at the rear. It weighed 11 tonnes and had a crew of four. This particular one was probably taken from the factory and deployed as part of the last-ditch defences of Berlin. Even WWI-era tanks were used by the Germans in Berlin's defence.

BELOW: A German staff car burns as a Soviet T-34/85/1 tank of the 3rd Guards Tank Army drives through the Hindenburg Park in southwest Berlin on 28 April 1945. German attempts to escape to the west from the capital were doomed when elements from Konev's 1st Ukrainian Front and Zhukov's 1st Belorussian Front linked up near Potsdam and surrounded the city. For Berliners, both soldiers and civilians alike, the battle now became one of survival until the war ended. SS hitsquads roamed the city looking for deserters and would execute suspects without trial.

ABOVE: The crew of a 152mm (5.98in) M1935 howitzer in the streets of the city prepares to engage targets near the Reichstag in Berlin in April 1945. On a tracked carriage, the howitzer weighed 18,350kg (40,455lbs), had a muzzle velocity of 880m/s (962yds/sec) and fired a 48.9kg (107.8lb) shell to a maximum range of 26,975m (29,500yds). In the final stages of the battle for Berlin, Soviet gunners used this formidable weapon in a direct-fire role, firing over open sights at German strong points. The corner of the building opposite may have been preemptively targeted, as it would be a prime spot for snipers.

LEFT: Its barrel ringed with 'kills', one of three 88mm (3.46in) Flak 37 guns that were deployed to defend the Reichstag against air attack stands on the Königs-Platz in front of the gutted building. The guns may have been pressed into service in an anti-tank role as the Soviet 150th Division launched the final assault; however, the fact that they are undamaged suggests that the crews did not wish to die as heroes defending this potent symbol of Imperial Germany and the Third Reich. The gun's anti-aircraft role meant that crew protection was minimal, and as is clear from the photograph, the gun is in a very exposed position.

LEFT: The classic photograph of the Red Flag being raised on the Reichstag at 1345 hours 30 April 1945 by men of the 150th Division. Viktor Temin, the Soviet Army photographer who took the picture, had carried a flag for the occasion and hoped to reproduce a picture as powerful as that of the US Marines raising the Stars and Stripes on Mount Suribachi on Iwo Jima in February 1945. The Soviet censors obliged him to air brush the wrist of the soldier supporting the flag raiser – several looted German watches were strapped to it.

RIGHT: The crew of a IS-2 tank of the 150th Division samples German wine in the shadow of the Reichstag. At 0400 hours on 30 April, along with the 207th Division, the tanks of the 150th had crossed the Moltke Bridge over the Spree and captured the Ministry of Interior building. The final assault across the Königs-Platz in front of the Reichstag took them over an anti-tank ditch and past three 88mm (3.46in) Flak guns. By 2400 hours, they were just inside the Reichstag, as Stalin had ordered them.

RIGHT: A Soviet officer directs a column of 'Iosef Stalin' IS2 heavy tanks along the streets of the suburbs of Berlin in May 1945, the city's surrender only hours away. Tank descent troops are seated on the rear deck. The infantry would be invaluable in street fighting, as they could neutralise enemy anti-tank guns, while the tank provided powerful long-range support to an attack, with its main armament capable of knocking out any German blockhouses or strongpoints. The Soviet tank commanders used the 12.7mm (0.5in) DshK1938 turret-mounted heavy anti-aircraft machine gun with its optical sight to engage German positions on the ground.

LEFT: A Soviet ISU122 heavy assault gun enters the Berlin suburbs in May 1945. The ISU122 had a crew of five and the same gun as that fitted to the IS2 tank. This one is passing a grocery store which bears a slogan coined by Dr Josef Goebbels that reads 'Berlin remains German'. As the Soviet and Allied forces closed in on Germany in 1945, slogans exhorting or challenging the local civilian population were painted by the SS and Nazi Party functionaries.

RIGHT: A squad of Soviet soldiers commanded by Sergeant Gorbatov stalks snipers in central Berlin in May 1945. The mixed dress of the group – the soldiers in *dvubortnaya vatnaya kurtka* (short quilted jacket) and *pilotka* (side hats), and the formally dressed NCO in *furazha* (peaked cap) and tunic with shoulder boards – and the fact that none wears a steel helmet suggest that either the photograph was posed after the fighting was over or it was taken very late in the action when the rest of the city had surrendered to the Soviets.

LEFT: A Soviet SU76M light self-propelled gun covers a crossroads in Berlin in May 1945. With its open top and rear, cramped turret area and general lack of crew comforts, the SU76M was not popular with its four-man crews; however, with the exception of the T-34 tank, it was the most widely produced armoured vehicle in the Soviet Union during World War II. Armed with a 76.2mm (3.0in) Zis-3 field gun, it had a maximum speed of 45km/h (30mph) and a range of 320km (199 miles), with armour protection of between 10mm (0.39in) and 35mm (1.38in). In common with other self-propelled guns, by the end of the war the SU76M was used in the direct fire role, using its armament to knock out German machine gun nests and other strongpoints.

ABOVE: Soviet infantry seated on an SU100 scan the upper windows of apartments in central Berlin in May 1945. The SU100, like the SU85 and the SU152, did not have secondary armament, so the crews of these assault gun crews relied on local infantry for defence against German infantry tank hunters. By the end of the war, many members of the *Volksturm*, the German militia, were armed (if they were armed at all) with a single *Panzerfaust* anti-tank rocket, so the danger to the vehicle was real enough. The crew of the SU100 in the foreground of the picture has dispensed with the spare fuel tanks on the rear hull and added an ammunition box as a stowage bin on the mudguard.

LEFT: A small group of German women and children make their way eastwards from the Brandenburg Gate down Unter-den-Linden in May 1945, following the surrender of the city. For the citizens of Berlin, 44 years would pass before the city was again the German capital and no longer divided and occupied by the Soviet Union, United States, United Kingdom and France. For the survivors left in Berlin, the first years after May 1945 would be particularly grim. The city had been hit by 29 major air raids, fought through and the Soviet soldiers who occupied it were (initially) brutal victors. Even those in the part occupied by the Western Allies struggled for food.

CHAPTER THIRTEEN

A Land Laid Bare

War, Plague, Pestilence and Famine

The suffering inflicted on the Soviet Union in World War II was staggering. Accurate figures for overall losses, however, took decades to emerge in the post-1945 Cold War world. As many as 27 million people may have died, the vast majority being civilians in the western republics of the Baltic, Belorussia and the Ukraine. In the 900-day siege of Leningrad, at least 635,000 people died and there were reports of cannibalism, as the starving inihabitants desperately sought to survive. In the liberated areas, the NKVD executed and deported suspected collaborators and even whole populations such as the Crimean Tartars. Hundreds of thousands died in the Gulags of Siberia in the 1940s and 1950s.

The Ukraine suffered particularly harshly. For every town such as Oradour in France or Lidice in Czechoslovakia that was destroyed, some 250 towns in the Ukraine were burned or blown up and their inhabitants murdered. Some 16,000 industrial plants and 28,000 collective farms were destroyed and direct material damage constituted over 40 per cent of the Soviet Union's wartime losses. By the end of the war, starvation, executions and death in combat had killed more than seven million Ukrainians.

The mines, farms, factories and the transport infrastructure in the western Soviet Union had been destroyed twice over – in the 'Scorched Earth' demolition operations of Soviet withdrawals in 1941 and 1942, and the subsequent German retreat from 1943 to 1945. Among the major casualties were the Dnepropetrovsk hydroelectric dam that supplied power to the Donets industrial region and the oil installations at Maikop.

Disruption was also caused by the massive industrial relocation programme. Some 2593 plants, together with their

LEFT: In 1942, horses graze in the stark wasteland of the western suburbs of Stalingrad, as a survivor guards her few possessions rescued from fires that have engulfed the area.

FAR LEFT: The original caption for this photograph states that it is Kiev women grieving at the news at the beginning of the Great Patriotic War. It may, in fact, be a montage.

key personnel, were moved from the western Soviet Union to the Volga region, the Urals and even Kazakhstan. Here, they were out of range of the Luftwaffe and thus continued to supply the Red Army with tanks, artillery and small arms. Workers in heavy industry, many of whom were women or juveniles, received a food ration allowance of 3181 to 4418 calories, while ordinary workers received between 1074 and 1176 calories. Dependants, however, were at almost starvation levels on 780 calories. 'Of these people,' said an editorial in *Soviet War News* in 1942, 'you can make everything – nails, tanks, poetry, victory.'

The material losses inflicted by the war are harder to estimate, but 1710 cities and 70,000 villages were partially or completely erased. By 1945, some 30 per cent of the national wealth had been destroyed.

The total demographic losses in the Soviet Union, including premature deaths and miscarriages, as well as desertion and emigration, are probably in the region of 48 million people, while a further two and a half million young men and women were deported to Germany as forced labour throughout the war.

For the Soviet leader, Stalin, however, the colossal human sacrifices of the war in the East were summed up simply and brutally. 'A single death is a tragedy,' he said, 'but a million deaths are a statistic.'

A RACIAL WAR

When Germany launched Operation Barbarossa, it was described as a *Rassenkampf*, a 'race war' between subhuman Slavs (*Untermenschen*) and superior Aryans (*Ubermenschen*).

The *Kommissar Erlass* (special orders) issued by Hitler stated that Commissars, the Soviet *politicheskii, rukovoditel,* or *politruk* (the political officers attached to the Red Army), 'hold views directly opposite to those of National Socialism. Hence these commissars must be eliminated! When captured in battle or in resistance are on principle to be disposed of by gunshot immediately.'

As the three German Army Groups penetrated into the Soviet Union at the beginning of Operation Barbarossa, they were followed by four *Einsatzgruppen* (Task Forces): A, B, C and D. Four of five *Einsatzkommandos* of company strength were subordinated below them. Staffed by men of the SIPO (State and Criminal Police) and the SD, their missions were operations against 'individuals hostile to the Reich'. In fact, their task was the wholesale execution of Jews, intellectuals and Communist functionaries. At Kiev, a total of 33,000 Jewish men, women and children were taken to the ravine at Babi Yar outside the city and machine-gunned to death by an *Einsatzgruppe*. In a year in the East, the firing squads of the *Einsatzgruppen* had killed at least 900,000 people.

Even the survival rate for Soviet soldiers who had surrendered was low. Five-sixths of the five and a quarter million Red Army soldiers taken prisoner by the Germans were dead by 1945. The long distances and climate did not favour the exhausted or wounded men's survival as they marched west. In the summer, the long columns of prisoners were marched across the dry steppe and many died from dehydration. Some were simply shot as a matter of course.

In the first winter of the war, German soldiers took the felt boots, hats and coats of captured or dead Soviet soldiers, since they themselves were inadequately dressed. In sub-zero temperatures, the Russian prisoners of war were doomed.

BELOW: A German propaganda photograph, showing the rural idyll being created by the land of the East being recolonised by 'ethnically pure' people of Germanic stock. The eventual intent was to clear large swathes of land of their former owners, who would either be 'disposed of' or used as slave labour for the further glory of the Third Reich.

ABOVE: A Russian woman conscripted to assist in the building of defensive positions labours alongside a German soldier. Civilians were used as labour by both sides. On a restricted, near-starvation diet, they were required to dig trenches, bunkers and anti-tank ditches in all weathers. Many in German hands died from these exertions. Himmler even stated that Russian women dying digging an anti-tank ditch was of no concern to him – what mattered was that the ditch was completed.

Incredibly, there were Soviet soldiers and civilians who were prepared to assist the Germans and even don Wehrmacht uniform. Some did so to survive and others out of a genuine hatred for the Soviet Union. A group of anti-Stalin Russian soldiers and politicians, the *Smolensker Komitee*, dropped leaflets behind Soviet lines and made broadcasts urging Russian soldiers to desert.

Soviet soldiers attached to German Army units were known as *Hilfswillige* (Hiwi), literally 'helpers'. By the end of 1943, it was not uncommon for a German battalion to contain a company of Hiwis working as drivers and even crewing weapons.

The *Ostlegion* was a more formalised group and consisted of six legions drawn from ethnic groups from Armenia, Azerbaijan, Georgia, North Caucasus, Turkmenistan and the Volga. There was also a cavalry corps composed of Kalmyks and a Crimean Tartar formation. The Vlasov Army, a force of two divisions and its commander Lieutenant General Andrey Vlasov, was used by the Germans for propaganda and only saw action at the close of the war. Finally, enough Cossacks volunteered to serve in the German armed forces to make up RONA, the 15th Cossack cavalry corps. Some of the Cossacks were actually Ukrainians. They were used in anti-partisan operations in France and Italy, and, at the close of the war, captured Cossacks were returned to the Soviet forces in Austria and also to certain death. All were doomed if they were captured alive by the Red Army.

Those Soviet prisoners who reached Poland and Germany were housed in 'POW Work Camps' and used as slave labour in munitions factories, mines and in the construction of the defences of the Atlantic Wall. Worked for long hours, on starvation rations, many died. The prisoners of war were joined by two and a half million Soviet citizens who were deported to Germany for forced labour and known as *Ostarbeiter* (eastern worker), identified by an armband with the letter 'O'. *Ostarbeiter* were employed in dangerous or exhausting work, including the construction of defences such as the Atlantic Wall. They had poor rations and those who attempted to escape were often hanged publicly as a deterrent to other workers.

In casual conversation in January 1942, Hitler remarked, 'Our guiding principle must be that these people [the Russians] have but one justification for existence – to be of use to us economically. In the field of public health there is no need whatsoever to extend to the subject races the benefit of our knowledge.'

In January 1945, Soviet forces fighting in Poland discovered the surviving sick and feeble inmates of the Auschwitz extermination camp. The establishment and operation of the extermination at camps such as Auschwitz-Birkenau, Belzec, Maidanek, Sobibor, Chelmno and Treblinka were the 'logical' outcome of the policy of mass executions begun by the *Einsatzgruppen*. Although some prisoners were shot, hanged, beaten to death, savaged by guard dogs, electrocuted or thrown to their deaths from the top of quarries, the majority of those who died were killed in the gas chambers.

New arrivals at the camps who had been deemed unfit for work were escorted to the *Brausebäder* (shower baths), where, after undressing, they were packed into the windowless bunker. To kill them, SS staff poured Zyklon-B, an amethyst blue crystal, through hatches in the roof. In contact with air, Zyklon-B formed hydrocyanic gas. The Auschwitz Commandant Rudolf Höss said that it took between three and fifteen minutes to kill everyone in the death chamber, depending on the weather conditions. 'We knew when the people were dead because their screaming stopped. We usually waited for half-an-hour before we opened the doors and removed the bodies.'

The concentration camps were the most powerful evidence of the Nazi policy of extermination of Jews, Romanies, homosexuals, Poles, Ukrainians and Soviet prisoners. More than 16 million people were murdered at extermination camps and by *Einsatzgruppen* in Russia. It was the fear of Soviet revenge for these murderous policies that kept many German soldiers fighting in the East.

ABOVE: The moment of death as bullets strike men condemned to death for their race, political convictions or simply as revenge. In the trench below them are earlier victims of an *Einsatzgruppe* (Task Force) in action in Russia.

ABOVE: The village of Lidice in the former Czechoslovakia burns in revenge for the assassination of Reinhard Heydrich, the Nazi 'Protector of Bohemia and Moravia' in Prague on 27 May 1942. All the inhabitants were systematically wiped out before the village was razed to the ground. Today a memorial stands on the spot.

LEFT: Cossack troops in German service gallop past for a dramatic propaganda photograph. Magazines such as *Signal* made much play of the variety of ethnic groups who had formerly lived in the Soviet Union, but who had now sided with Germany in her battle against the Bolsheviks. Some of these 'volunteers' had signed up to escape almost certain death as prisoners of war, but others had real grievances against Stalin and the Soviet Union.

ABOVE: Soviet troops of the 1st Ukrainian Front march through the gutted streets of Vinnitza in the Ukraine on 20 March 1944. They are passing an abandoned German Army or administrative office. The Ukraine that had welcomed the Germans was brutally exploited by them. It was stripped of raw materials and agricultural produce, and nearly four million young men and women were kidnapped and used as *Ostarbeiter* slave workers in the armaments industries in Germany and Poland.

BELOW: A German prisoner of war, in a column of prisoners under a light Soviet escort, glances at the body of one of the last defenders of the Third Reich in April 1945. In many cases the *Waffen-SS* fought to the last in the East knowing that they might well be executed if captured. Other men whose entire families had been killed in air raids had nothing more to lose and were prepared to kill as many of the enemy as they could until they themselves were killed.

LEFT: The celebrated Soviet film director Alexander P. Dovjenko, decorated with the title Honoured Film Director of the USSR, sits in the hatch of a PzKpfw VI Tiger Ausf E which was probably captured in the fighting at Kursk in 1943. Under Stalin, every aspect of Soviet life was used in assisting in the defeat of Nazi Germany. The fight was presented as patriotic rather than political and the emphasis was put on defending the historical 'Mother Russia', rather than the Soviet Union.

BELOW: F. I. Udin, a pipe-smoking Soviet war photographer working for the 1st Ukrainian Front newspaper *Za Chest Rodiny* ('For the Honour of Fatherland'), sizes up a scene of destruction at Vinnitza main railway station in the Ukraine on 20 March 1944. Udin's choice of a pipe is a practical solution to smoking the harsh Russian tobacco – if paper was available, a cigarette could be rolled; without it, the pipe was a good working substitute. The upturned truck bears mute tribute to the hugely destructive bombardments that were a hallmark of Soviet offensive operations.

ABOVE: Trucks deliver a work detail to the chaos of destruction in Stalingrad in the spring of 1943. The task of reconstruction was daunting and much of the heavy work was undertaken by women or prisoners of war. The Soviet Union retained some of its prisoners until the mid-1950s – some because they were senior officers, but many so that they could be used as labourers.

RIGHT: With her husband conscripted into the army, a Ukrainian woman stands alone and desolate in the smouldering ruins of her home in 1941. The original caption for this photograph says that the Germans burned the building, but it could equally have been burned by retreating Red Army soldiers or hit by artillery fire. Many rural homes were built from timber and had thatch roofs, which made them terribly vulnerable – only the fireplace and chimney were made from stone or brick.

INDEX

Page numbers in *italics* refer to captions.